Japanese Literati Painters

The Third Generation

by Penelope E. Mason

The Brooklyn Museum

This publication is made possible by a grant from the Mary Livingston Griggs and Mary Griggs Burke Foundation

Published for the exhibition
Japanese Literati Painters:
The Third Generation
The Brooklyn Museum: Oriental Art Special Exhibition Gallery
June 15–August 14, 1977

Front Cover:
Spring Thoughts While Watching a Fisherman 1844
Nukina Kaioku (1778–1863)
Collection: Mrs. Jackson Burke
Catalogue number 18

Edited by Libby W. Seaberg.
Designed and published by The Brooklyn Museum,
Division of Publications and Marketing Services,
Eastern Parkway, Brooklyn, New York 11238.
Printed in the USA by The Falcon Press, Philadelphia.

ISBN 0-87273-061-1

Preface & Acknowledgements

The germ of the idea that grew into this exhibition of Japanese literati painting was planted in the minimuseum of Mr. and Mrs. Jackson Burke in the late spring of 1974. I had stopped by on some errand now long forgotten and as usual was invited into the minimuseum to see their latest acquisition, in this case *Landscapes of the Four Seasons* by Yamamoto Baiitsu. We stood in front of the paintings for a long while talking about them, studying details and finally just appreciating them in silence. They seemed to me then and even now to be four of the most beautiful paintings I have ever seen. I could not help but be struck by the discrepancy between the quality of these paintings and the standard appraisal of Baiitsu as an inferior literati artist. In one Japanese text he is discussed under the heading "Deterioration: the Nagoya Painters." Clearly, here was an artist who merited investigation and reappraisal.

The opportunity to study Baiitsu and the other Nanga artists active in the first half of the nineteenth century came last autumn when I taught a graduate seminar on Japanese literati painting at Yale University. So that the class might have the opportunity to study these later artists by looking at some original examples of their work rather than by having to depend entirely on photographs, an exhibition was organized at the Yale Art Gallery, and each of the students undertook the writing of label copy and essays on one or two of the artists included in the show. Some of the entries in the present catalogue reflect their work: Donna Albright's essay on Okada Beisanjin, Hongnam Kim's research on Nakabayashi Chikutō, Barbara Okada's writing on Yamamoto Baiitsu and Hine Taizan, and Emiko Staubitz's study of Tanomura Chikuden and Takahashi Sōhei. Stimulated by the availability of original works of art, the students set as their primary goal the honing of their skills at analyzing the composition and brush techniques of individual paintings. In the process of looking at, and of discussing and arguing about the works and the artists we were studying, the class grew to have a great respect for the unique contributions of each of its individual members.

The Burkes' afforded me not only the visual experience that led to this exhibition, but Mrs. Jackson Burke has also provided the encouragement and support that made it possible. For these kindnesses I am deeply grateful. Conscious as she is of the importance of conserving the works that she has been priviledged to acquire, she also believes strongly in making her collection available to students and consequently allowed her paintings to come to the Yale Gallery well in advance of their public display so that the students would have ample opportunity to study them during the course of the semester.

I would also like to express my appreciation to the others who have lent paintings to this exhibition: an anonymous lender—a collector whose enthusiasm for Japanese art knows no bounds, a friend with whom I have often looked at paintings and talked about them into the wee hours of the morning—Dr. and Mrs. Kurt Gitter and the New Orleans Museum of Art, David M. Okada, and Michael Fox and Robin Fox Cunningham.

In order that a permanent record of the exhibition be made, the Mary Livingston Griggs and the Mary Griggs Burke Foundation donated the funds necessary for the production of this catalogue. In addition, I received the aid and encouragement of two Yale colleagues, Professor Fu Shen of the Department of the History of Art, who helped me decipher several difficult colophons and obscure seals, and Parker Huang of the Department of East Asian Languages and Literatures, whose sensitive explication of the Chinese poems by Nukina Kaioku helped me enormously in rendering them into appropriate English. However, the contributions of colleagues and students notwithstanding, any errors in this text are solely my responsibility. Finally my thanks go to Robert Moes, Curator of Oriental Art at The Brooklyn Museum, who gave the Yale exhibition its second incarnation.

Introduction

The school of painting in Japan known as literati, or to use the Japanese terms, Bunjinga ("scholar's painting") or Nanga ("southern painting"), came into existence around the year 1700; reached a peak of mature, accomplished expression within sixty to seventy-five years; and lost completely its once fresh and innovative spirit by the time of the Meiji Restoration in 1868. The term *literati* was applied to this school of painting not because its practitioners were all members of the intelligentsia, although a number of them were, but rather because the source of inspiration for Japanese literati artists was the work of gentlemen-scholars on the continent.

The literati class in China was fostered by a system, developed in the Han Dynasty (206 B.C.–222 A.D.), of Confucian education, which aimed at the perfection of the intellect and the preparation of students to pass the examinations that would qualify them to occupy administrative positions within the government. However, the successful completion of Chinese civil service tests was not quite what we think of today as adequate proof of administrative ability. These tests measured the examinee's knowledge of history and his ability to explicate passages from the Confucian classics and to write, in an appropriate style of calligraphy, lucid prose and lyric poetry. The brush with which the Chinese wrote was considered to be an extension of the hand animated by the soul. Thus, one's calligraphic style was an index to one's character. Those students who passed the civil service examinations were among the best-educated men in the country; they were true scholars, with the cultural accoutrements of the genteel class. Yet at the same time they were amateurs, essentially untrained for their intended profession and unable, because of the demands of their careers, to practice their artistic skills except in their spare time for their own amusement. Their amateur status, particularly with regard to the arts, became an essential element in their attitude toward creative expression.

In the Han Dynasty painting was not considered a necessary accomplishment for the gentleman-scholar, but by the eleventh century it had become intimately related with the arts of poetry and calligraphy, especially in the thinking of the influential group of literati who gathered around the poet-painter-administrator Su Shih, or as he is better known by his art name, Su Tung-p'o. These men would gather for a drinking party and in the course of the evening one or two might paint pictures depicting, for example, the "Four Gentlemen"—the bamboo, the plum, the orchid, and the chrysanthemum—a set of pictorial themes that depended for their effect on simple, but controlled and refined brush work. Others in the party might compose poems to be inscribed upon the paintings. The criteria for judging the quality of the painting was primarily the character of the man who created it and the circumstances under which it was executed. Su Tung-p'o once inscribed on a painting:

> Looking at scholars' painting is like judging the best horse of the empire, one sees how spirit has been brought out; but when it comes to artisan painters, one usually just gets whip and skin, stable and fodder, without a speck of superior achievement. After looking at a few feet or so one is tired.[1]

Clearly, in Su Tung-p'o's day it was not the style of a painting that established its quality but the fact that it was the expression of a member of the literati class. Furthermore, because these paintings were personal statements made for friends, the artists never sold them but simply gave them away.

By the fourteenth century a definite "literati" style of painting had emerged. The country was ruled by Mongols, who did not trust the Chinese and did not allow the literati class to play a significant role in the government. Consequently, many scholars remained in the cultural centers of the south and devoted much more of their time to painting and to calligraphy. Gradually, through the work of Chao Meng-fu and the four great masters of the latter part of the Yuan Dynasty (1260–1368), Ni Tsan, Huang Kung-wang, Wu Chen, and Wang Meng, an approach to painting was developed that depended on such technical elements as light washes of ink, calligraphic outlines, and textural strokes for facilitating the quick execution of a work so as to capture the quality of a particular scene and the mood of the man experiencing it.

The next step in the evolution of literati art in China was the classification by Tung Ch'i-ch'ang (1555–1636) of all Chinese artists into two schools, using as his model the philosophies of the two main branches of Ch'an or Zen Buddhism: the Northern, which believed in gradual progress toward spiritual enlightenment; and the Southern, which put credence in a sudden intuitive understanding of the nature of reality. According to Tung's theory, scholar-painters regardless of where they came from in China belonged to the Southern school, *Nan-tsung hua* (or in Japanese, *Nanshū-ga*, most commonly abbreviated to Nanga), because they were men of high character and their paintings were spontaneous, intuitive, and highly personal expressions. They also reflected the education of the artist through their references to antiquity and his status as an amateur rather than professional painter through their deliberately awkward quality.

There is an interesting paradox in Tung's theory, namely, that the Confucian scholar dedicated to the preservation of knowledge and committed to the concept of the perfectability of the intellect through study should espouse in his artistic creations an aesthetic of sudden enlightenment and immediate expression. The answer lies in the dislike Tung and his colleagues felt for professionalism and commercialism in the arts. Painting and calligraphy were the pastimes of the genteel class, vehicles for expressing their feelings, windows into their character. The painting that was meticulously constructed and carefully executed could not possibly serve the same function. However, to express oneself through painting required skill. The fact that one had used a brush since childhood for writing letters did not mean that one could automatically create the complex landscapes made possible by the stylistic innovations of Yuan Dynasty artists, no matter how willing one's spirit might be. For the scholar there could be only one way of acquiring such technical knowledge—the study of the work of other literati artists. Thus, paintings rather than nature became the object of later paintings.[2] A logical outgrowth of this trend was the production of instructional manuals on painting, such as the *Pa-chung Hua-p'u* (in Japanese the *Hasshū Gafu*), or *Eight Different Painting Albums,* produced in 1620 during Tung's own lifetime, and the *Chieh-tzu-yuan Hua-chuan* (in Japanese the *Kashien Gaden*), or *The Mustard Seed Garden Manual of Painting.* The latter was published between 1679 and 1701, the first volume appearing at the earlier date, the second and third coming out after the turn of the century. Tung's theories had another important effect on Chinese literati painting: they split the movement into two factions—the orthodox literati, who constructed their paintings according to set formulas, and the eccentrics, several of them Ch'an monks, who tried to maintain a degree of spontaneity in their work and who attempted to capture the essence of a particular natural scene.

At the time Tung Ch'i-ch'ang was enunciating his theories of painting, Japan was becoming an isolated country. The Tokugawa regime, which had come to power in the early 1600s after a prolonged period of civil strife, wanted to close Japan off from disruptive foreign influences, particularly Christianity, which had taken root in Kyushu and western Honshu and had resulted in several bloody peasant uprisings against the central government. Furthermore, wanting to establish a monopoly on the profits from commerce with the outside world, the Tokugawa regime, in effect, closed the country to foreigners by restricting them to the port of Nagasaki, which was privately controlled by the Tokugawa, and by banning the importation of books and other carriers of foreign culture.

A second element of Tokugawa policy, one that prepared the way for a cultural rapprochement with China, was the espousal of Confucianism as the philosophical basis for governing the country. The motive behind this was that Confucianism appeared to the Tokugawa shogunate to offer a system of interrelationships that would guarantee internal political stability. Confucianism postulated a theory of government that held that the ruler, be he shogun or daimyo, had a responsibility to govern for the benefit of his people, whose members, in turn, had a duty to fulfill their functions and obligations within the society. As the doctrine of Confucianism was adapted to fit the Japanese context, the samurai provided the model for the ideal human being, a man who maintained his martial skills but who also cultivated his aptitudes for administration and for learning. A Confucian academy was established in Edo, modern-day Tokyo, the seat of the Tokugawa government, and in the *han,* or fief, schools Confucian principles were taught to the children of samurai serving in daimyo administrations. Gradually, men who had once lived by the sword were converted into bureaucrats and the government was able to keep peace for nearly three hundred years.

It need hardly be said that the Japanese samurai-administrators were not as well educated as their Chinese counterparts and because of their military background and pragmatic attitudes toward life had little sense of the value of poetry or art as vehicles for personal expression. They were clearly not true literati in the Chinese sense. The first samurai to devote time to painting were punished by their feudal lords for debauchery. However, because of the high value they placed on Confucian thought, the Japanese gradually became aware of the Chinese concept of the literatus and of the art associated with the literati class. On the other hand, because there was no strong tradition of the poet-painter-scholar in Japan, literati painting did not become the preserve of any single class; it was available to a much wider variety of intellects and painting talents—samurai; *rōnin,* or samurai who had renounced their positions within the feudal system and the stipends accruing to those positions; haiku poets; and even professional painters of the merchant class. In Japan it was the style of the painting and the character of its expression, not the status of its artist, that determined the painting's value as a work of art. Furthermore, there was no stigma attached to selling one's works or to painting on commission. In the Japanese context the amateur status of the painter and his disdain for commercialism were irrelevancies for all but a few practitioners of the style.

Because of the restrictions on the importation of foreign books and on the travel of foreigners within Japan, knowledge of Chinese literati painting came to Japan in a distinctly fragmentary way. Between the late seventeenth and the beginning of the nineteenth centuries, the most important vehicles for the transmission of this knowledge were undoubtedly the block-printed painting manuals, such as *The Eight Different Picture Albums* and *The Mustard Seed Garden Manual of Painting*, which offered models for depicting plants, trees, rocks, mountains, and human figures in the styles of various Chinese masters. Rather soon after its publication in China, each of these works found its way to Japan, and the demand for each was such that new editions were quickly prepared for publication, that of *The Eight Albums* in 1671 and that of *The Mustard Seed Garden Manual* in 1748.

Obaku Zen priest-painters who emigrated from China to Japan after the founding of the Ch'ing Dynasty in 1644 provided a second source of information. Priests such as Yin-yuan and his successor at the temple of Mampukuji Mu-an were probably the first direct contact the Japanese had with contemporary Chinese painting. Many of these priests, in addition to being knowledgeable on religious matters, were also amateur painters working in the literati and Zen styles prevalent in their native regions.

In addition, Chinese merchants in Nagasaki who dabbled in calligraphy and landscape painting for pleasure and professional painters who sojourned briefly in that port city brought the Japanese into direct contact with Nanga and other contemporary styles of Chinese art. Foremost of the amateur painters was I Hai, who came to Japan in 1720 and for the next thirty years conducted trading missions between China and Japan. His painting style was directly related to Tung Ch'i-ch'ang and the orthodox school that continued the conservative side of his teachings. The most important of the professional painters was Shen Ch'uan, or Shen Nan-p'in, who arrived in Japan in 1731 and stayed for about two years.

However, each of these three sources had inherent weaknesses as bearers of knowledge of Chinese literati painting. The Obaku priests, for example, were not strongly interested in Nanga landscapes per se but rather in subjects related to Zen or in themes like the "Four Gentlemen." As for the Nagasaki enclave, none of its members was a first-rate painter. Only Shen Nan-p'in was a trained professional, and

he worked not in the literati style, but in the brilliantly colored, minutely detailed, realistic style of bird and flower painting popular in China in the Ming and Ch'ing dynasties. The manuals on painting were deficient as a source of information because they were illustrated with wood-block prints, a medium for reproducing the techniques of painting which requires that the building up of brush strokes—darker, wetter ink strokes over lighter, drier sketch lines—to achieve a rich blend of shades be reduced to single lines that will stand out in sharp contrast to the white background paper. So pervasive was the influence of these block-printed manuals that it was not until the early nineteenth century that Japanese artists learned to work in the true Chinese manner of building up brush strokes to achieve surface texture.

The factor accounting for this change in Nanga painting was the exposure of Japanese artists to actual works of art produced on the continent. Since most of these works came into the country through private channels, it is very difficult today to evaluate the authenticity and the quality of the paintings that Japanese artists chose to study and of the actual sources of the stylistic elements they elected to incorporate into their own work. Some Nanga painters have indicated in inscriptions on their works that they were imitating the style of Tung Yuan, Mi Fu, Ni Tsan and Huang Kung-wang, as well as of lesser-known artists, but it seems much more likely from the paintings themselves that Japanese knowledge of the Chinese masters was filtered through the perceptions of Ming and Ch'ing painters working in the styles traditionally associated with their names. Nevertheless, Japanese artists, particularly those of the third generation, thought that they were studying original works and that they were in touch with the geniune life spirit of a particular Chinese master; indeed, their own paintings are much closer to the Chinese than was the work of earlier artists. The primary factor that differentiates one generation of Nanga artists from another is the caliber of information each had about Chinese literati painting.

In some ways the development of Nanga painting in Japan, which took place within a period of 150 years, has elements in common with the much longer evolution of literati painting in China. However, from the above discussion it should be clear that the traditions in the two countries were so different that one cannot draw precise parallels. Nevertheless, certain similarities can be noted. The first men to take up literati painting were samurai, the Japanese counterpart of the Chinese literati class. Two members of this group were Yanagisawa Kien (1706–1758) and Gion Nankai (1677–1751), who were encouraged to experiment with pictorial expression because of their Confucian training. Thus they, like Su

Tung-p'o and the other scholars in his circle, turned to painting as a vehicle for personal expression, and it must be added that the Japanese artists who first studied the art of literati painting did so because they were aware that this was an ideal of the Chinese gentleman-scholar. These two artists worked primarily from the painting manuals, executing rather stiff versions of the "Four Gentlemen" and narrow vertical landscapes of a clearly composite nature—a rock and tree formation in the style of Ni Tsan, a background mountain in the manner of Huang Kung-wang.

The exception to the rule among the Nanga pioneers was Sakaki Hyakusen, a commercial artist born in Nagoya to a family, probably of Chinese origins, that was in the pharmaceutical business. Through its professional contacts in China, namely, the exporters of Chinese medicines for sale in Nagoya, his family was able to provide Hyakusen with a much broader exposure to Chinese literati painting than was available to his contemporaries. A recent study of his work has demonstrated that his familiarity with continental painting far exceeded anything he might have learned through the available manuals of painting.[3] He was an artist of considerable talent, capable of working in a number of different styles—a facile *haiga* style of rapidly sketched, humorous paintings illustrating haiku themes, large-scale panel and screen paintings in a heavy monochromatic style, realistic landscapes—in addition to the newly introduced literati style of painting. He was also a haiku poet of some skill. In many ways he foreshadowed the artists of the second generation. Nanga was merely a style for Hyakusen: its techniques and its themes provided him with fresh inspiration, but the life-style of its continental adherents did not concern him.

The second generation of Nanga artists, particularly Ikeno Taiga (1723–1776) and Yosa Buson (1716–1783), may be compared to the four great masters of the Yuan Dynasty in the sense that they developed Japanese Nanga painting into a distinct and fully realized statement. Taiga incorporated a great many influences into his work: the decorative style of the Rimpa school founded by Sōtatsu and Ogata Kōrin; the monochrome ink styles of the Muromachi period—some of his paintings have been compared to the work of the Zen monk Josetsu; and even the perspective of Western art, which was becoming known in Japan through Dutch copper-plate etchings. However, the primary element from which he developed his personal style was the technique of illustration found in the woodblock-printed painting manuals. He re-translated into ink and color the dots and hard outlines to which complex Chinese brush techniques had been reduced for woodblock-print reproduction and he painted these strokes either in bright colors or in ink over thin washes of color. His knowledge of Chinese painting styles and themes clearly exceeded that of most of the first generation of Nanga artists, but like Hyakusen, he was a commercial painter with a primarily visual orientation toward his work. He felt no particular need to adopt the life-style of the Chinese literati in order to utilize those elements of their manner of painting that suited his artistic purposes. The same can be said of his contemporary Yosa Buson, who was both a painter and a poet of great talent—he is usually ranked with Matsuo Bashō as one of the most accomplished haiku poets in Japan. It apears that he took up painting in the Nanga style in order to support himself while he concentrated on his poetry writing. Buson, like Taiga, used Chinese painting as a point of departure for his own paintings. He saw nothing wrong with presenting a classic Chinese theme such as moonlight on Mt. Omei, a famous mountain in China, in a new and fresh way, which suited the Japanese taste by employing the surprising juxtapositions of ideas peculiar to haiku poetry.

Perhaps the most significant difference between the second and third generations of Nanga artists was their general attitude toward Chinese culture. Whereas the second generation was informed, however fragmentarily, about Chinese culture, its members used it only as a point of departure, a source of inspiration, for their own creations. The third generation, on the other hand, particularly the Kyoto-Osaka artists grouped around Rai Sanyō, a noted Confucian scholar, espoused literati culture completely. In the manner of Tung Ch'i-ch'ang and his associates, these artists studied every Chinese painting to which they could gain access. They wrote treatises on literati painting theory, attempted to apply Tung Ch'i-ch'ang's criteria of Northern and Southern painting to Japanese art, and even tried to emulate the life-styles of the Chinese literati.

What they gained by this total commitment to the study of continental literati art was a new vocabulary of techniques for pictorial representation: new compositional formulas, different ways of drawing landscape motifs, and, above all, new methods for representing space and the relationship between objects. However, it is ironic that in devoting themselves so wholeheartedly to the study and emulation of Chinese culture, they lost the element that made Nanga painting in the hands of Taiga and Buson so vital, namely, the freedom to combine foreign and indigenous motifs in fresh and stimulating ways. That is not to say that the artists of the third generation were slavish imitators of Chinese styles, but that they did look to China exclusively for their inspiration instead of drawing as well on their native pictorial traditions.

An artist who stands on the border line between the second and third generation is Okada Beisanjin (1744–1820). Beisanjin apears to have been an orphan who, somehow by his early teens, had acquired a knowledge of Confucianism, which gave him the leverage to move from the job of tending ricefields to that of custodian of a rice warehouse in Osaka—a position that carried with it the rank of samurai—and finally to resign his post and retire to his scholar's study to read, write poetry, and paint in the company of his friends, a circle that included Rai Sanyō. As a painter Beisanjin was self-taught, and his style seems to have depended heavily on Chinese wood-block painting manuals for the depiction of mountains and figures, which in his paintings are outlined and given texture through the use of grey ink lines applied over washes of color. Thus, although he had access to the new Chinese paintings that were being studied by his literati friends and he aspired to the life-style of a Chinese literatus, he painted in a style closer in feeling to the second generation of artists than to the third.

His son Hankō (1802–1846), on the other hand, was one of the most accomplished of the third-generation artists. He began by studying painting under Beisanjin but soon moved on, in spite of his father's strong disapproval, to copy the Chinese paintings available to him and to incorporate elements from them into his own style. The names that appear on his paintings as sources of his style include Mi Fu, Wu Chen, Huang Kung-wang, Tung Ch'i-ch'ang, and Wang Hui. In his favorite painting format, the long vertical hanging scroll, he was able to create an impression of forms in light and shadow and a sense of atmosphere through the use of soft, colored or grey washes. Furthermore, his landscape motifs are placed in logical spatial relations to each other so that as the eye moves through his paintings from foreground to background, one has a strong feeling of recession into depth. The painting included in this exhibition, *The Farewell Gift,* is atypical in its format—it is a horizontal hanging scroll—but even within this format Hankō has been able to suggest both the space of a small village next to a lake and the cold smoke and pale leaden sky of January.

The other third-generation artist who succeeded admirably at depicting atmosphere and logical spatial relationships is the Nagoya painter Yamamoto Baiitsu (1783–1856). Best known for his bird and flower paintings, which, although repetitive in subject matter and composition, are superb examples of brush technique, Baiitsu painted landscapes that in their quality of light, mood of season, and shapes and forms are masterful recreations of a particular moment. It has been said that of all the third-generation Nanga artists, Baiitsu's

work alone could be mistaken for a Chinese painting, so complete was his assimilation of later continental literati styles.

The theorists of the third generation were Tanomura Chikuden (1777–1835) and Nakabayashi Chikutō (1776–1853). Of the two, Chikuden was probably the better-educated and more profound thinker, owing to his birth into the samurai class and to his early education in the Confucian academy on the fief on which his father served. Chikutō, on the other hand, was born to an obstetrician in Nagoya and seems to have received little formal training under the auspices of his parents. Instead, a wealthy merchant, Kamiya Ten'yū, helped him to begin his career as a Nanga painter. Eventually both Chikuden and Chikutō settled in the Kyoto area, joined the Rai Sanyō circle, and began to develop their theories of art. Chikuden in his *Guide to Literati Painting,* (*Bunga Yūeki*), stresses the importance of studying both the painting manuals and original works of art:

> It will benefit those who have just begun studying literati painting to read the *Chieh-tsu-yuan hua-chuan* (*The Mustard Seed Garden Manual of Painting*) so as to grasp the major concepts of landscape painting. Remember the terms for texture strokes and dotting techniques, and the names of the Southern school masters. As for study of brush and ink, it would be better to copy famous works of the Yuan and Ming, and those of the Ch'ing which are not vulgar, so as to understand their techniques. Terms such as "spirit harmony" or "remote harmony" spring to the lips to be changed immediately, but only after seeing the marvellous remains of ancient masters will they be understood naturally by the mind.[4]

Chikutō, on the other hand, investigated the Northern- and Southern-school theories of Tung Ch'i-ch'ang and attempted to apply Tung's criteria to Japanese painting as well. His early study of Chinese painting, *Gado Kongōsho,* published before he left Nagoya, reveals distinct lacunae in his knowledge of literati art. However, in Kyoto he had access to more reliable sources and his commentaries improved considerably. The standards he applied to Japanese art were extremely narrow, and he is known to have criticized Taiga for not painting in a more orthodox style and Buson for his frivolous attitude toward his art, presumably a reference to his illustration of haiku poems.

One element common to the painting of both men was a peculiar kind of nostalgia for the continent, which they had never seen, and for the life of the Chinese literatus. The painting by Chikuden included in this exhibition, *First Visit to the Red Cliffs,* suggests in its inscription that the artist on the anniversary of Su Tung-p'o's first excursion was so moved by the remembrance of this moment which had occurred centuries ago, that he set brush to paper and tried to re-create the image of the event. Nostalgia appears in Chikutō's work as well, in such paintings as the 1838 version of *Mountains and Valleys Deep and Far* in which he creates an idealized view of a Chinese landscape as though it were the daydreamed image of the scholar seated, in what is clearly a Japanese pavilion, in the foreground.

This sense of yearning to participate in the literati culture of China and the realization of the futility of such a desire are no more poignantly expressed than in the poem by Nukina Kaioku accompanying his painting *Spring Thoughts on Seeing a Fisherman.* The sake he receives on his daydreamed visit to China is given on credit—it is not something he can ever claim to own. The overwhelming impression one feels in studying these third-generation Nanga artists is that the closer they came to a true understanding of Chinese literati culture and art, the more cognizant they became of the gap between their own world and this foreign ideal to which they aspired.

1. Susan Bush, *The Chinese Literati on Painting: Su Shih (1037–1101) to Tung Ch'i-ch'ang (1555–1636)* (Cambridge, Mass., 1971), p. 29.

2. Joseph R. Levenson, "The Amateur Ideal in Ming and Early Ch'ing Society: Evidence from Painting," in *Chinese Thought and Institutions,* ed. John K. Fairbank (Chicago, 1957), p. 331.

3. James Cahill, "Sakaki Hyakusen no Kaiga," *Bijutsu Shi,* 24 (March 1976): 2.

4. Hsio-yen Shih, *Literati Paintings from Japan* (Hong Kong, 1974), p. 38.

Catalogue

NOTE
Dimensions throughout are in inches; height precedes width.

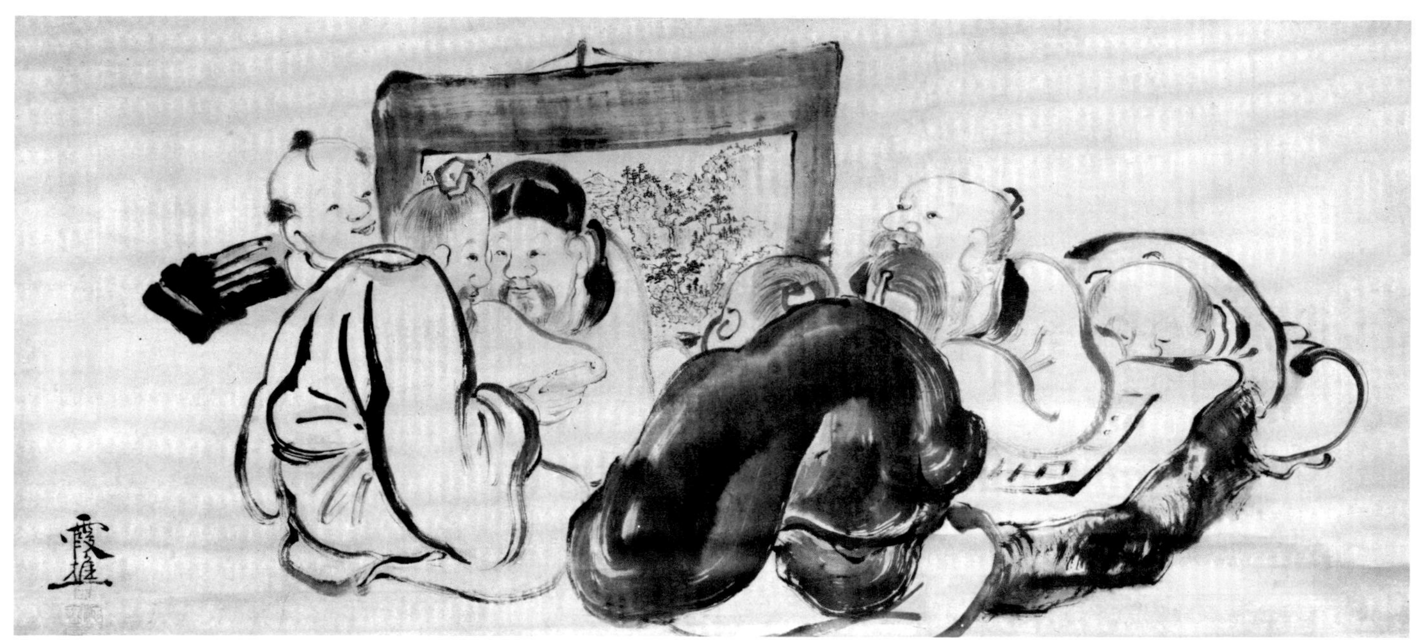

1 Scholars Conversing

Ikeno Taiga (1723–1776).
Hanging scroll, ink on paper, 22½ x 52¾.
Signature: Kashō (Half-blind woodcutter).
Seals: Rectangular intaglio seal "Sekitei."
Large square relief seal "Chi Mumei In."
Collection: Mrs. Jackson Burke.

Ikeno Taiga, a man of rather humble origins, was one of two artists of the second generation, Buson the other, who brought Japanese literati painting to a state of maturity. Taiga's knowledge of Chinese-style painting was derived from three principal sources: the teachings of the Obaku Zen monks at the temple of Mampukuji; woodblock-printed instructional texts, such as the *Eight Different Picture Albums* and the *Mustard Seed Garden Manual of Painting;* and Chinese paintings available to him in Japan. However, it was from the painting manuals that he derived one characteristic element of his style, the use of individual dots or brush strokes to delineate forms. When the complex brush techniques for painting rocks or mountains, human figures or foliage, were reduced to a series of lines cut in a printing block, this stippled kind of effect resulted. Taiga clearly had had access to genuine Chinese works in which he could see the literati manner of applying stroke over stroke to build up the surface texture of a painting, but he had chosen to develop the pointillist technique and to transmit it to his disciples.

In the painting *Scholars Conversing* a landscape screen painted in Taiga's dot-technique contrasts with the very free brush strokes and washes used to delineate the five scholars and the little boy who is peeking at them. The figures are treated with some degree of humor: one scholar looks intently at his companion, who is reading from a scroll, while another gazes into space, and a fourth has simply fallen asleep. Yet there is no attempt to satirize. These men are intellectuals, intent on the pursuit of ideas and skilled at the gentlemanly arts of music, writing, calligraphy, and painting.

The seals impressed on the painting were used by Taiga in the decade of the 1760s which would place this work in the artist's mature period, along with such well-known paintings as the *fusuma,* or sliding screen, of Henjōkō-in on Mt. Koya.

2   Ghostly Rocks and a Swiftly Flowing Waterfall

Aiseki (dates unknown).
Hanging scroll, ink and colors on paper, 52 x 22⅞.
Inscription: Ghostly Rocks and a Swiftly Flowing
                Waterfall, Aiseki.
Seal: Oval relief "Shinkei" (True Vow).
Collection: Mrs. Jackson Burke.

Little is known about the painter Aiseki except that he was a Buddhist monk, possibly of the Obaku sect, who may have studied directly with Taiga or else with a disciple of his. His style is reminiscent of the freedom and abbreviated statements of Taiga's late years, and it is tempting to think that he studied directly with the master.

The mood of *Ghostly Rocks and a Swiftly Flowing Waterfall* is made faintly disquieting by its swirling rock forms, yet the menace of the landscape is held in check by the decorative use of color, particularly in the trees in the lower part of the painting, and by the pointillist brush strokes, an element clearly derived from Taiga. In the foreground two groups of rocks arranged on a diagonal reach forward, like the forepaws of a giant animal, enclosing within their grasp a scholar and his servant. Above the trees that line the embankment are mountain shapes, one capped with a plateau, the other rounded at the top. As the eye moves upward, these two basic forms are repeated, but with increasing irrationality, until the climax of the painting is reached—a massive, sharply undercut peak, which , more like a cloud than a rock, seems to be shifting and re-forming. This shifting effect is achieved by applying over thin uneven washes of color, long, curving brush strokes, which convey a sense of movement, and is heightened by the white areas in the center, which seem to bear no relation to hard, solid rock forms. The painting creates a strong sense of the life force present in the natural world.

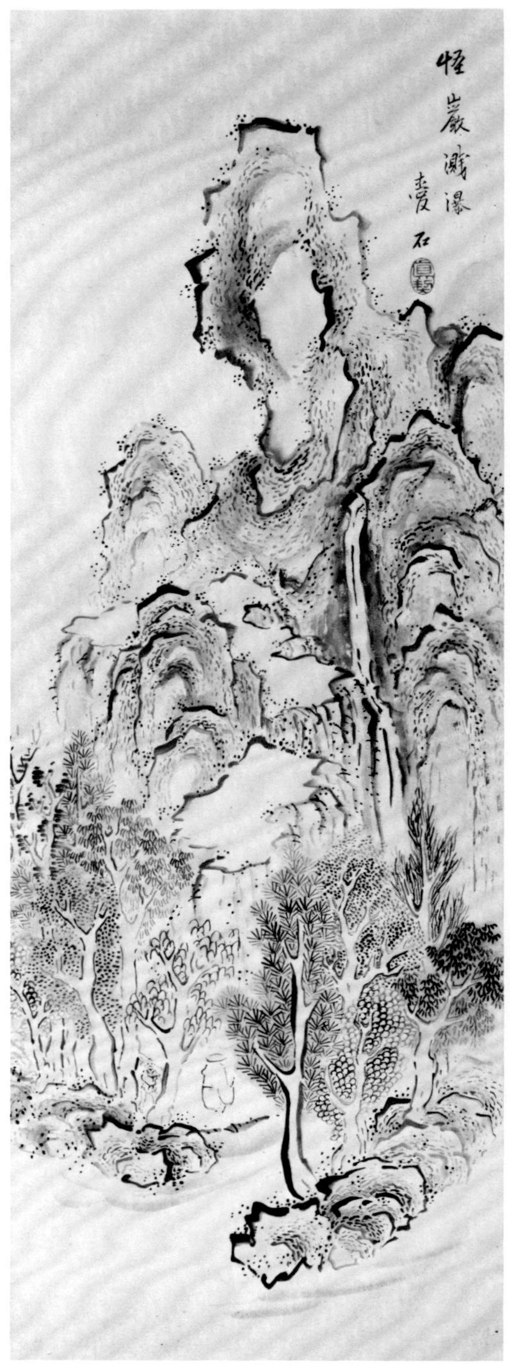

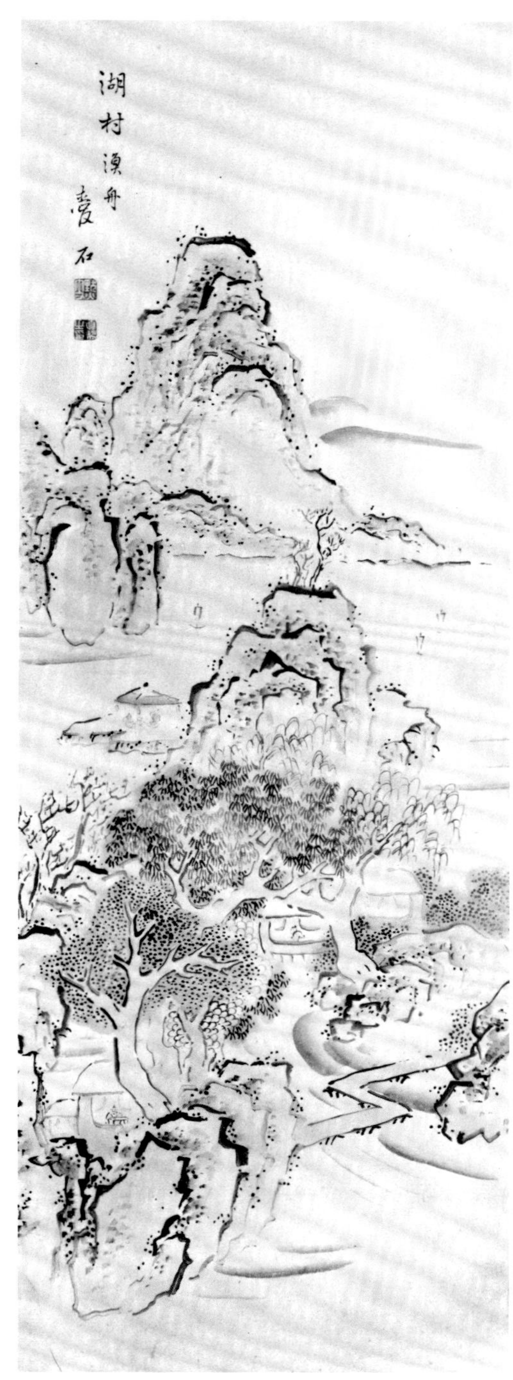

3   **A Lakeside Village and Scattered Boats**
Aiseki (dates unknown).
Hanging scroll, ink and colors on paper, 52 x 22⅞.
Inscription: Lake-side village, scattered boats, Aiseki.
Seals: Square intaglio seal ''Mokusō'' (Silent old man).
       Square intaglio seal ''Shinkei no In'' (Seal of
       True Vow).
Collection: Mrs. Jackson Burke.

The mood of this painting is much more lighthearted than its mate, *Ghostly Rocks and a Swiftly Flowing Waterfall* (see no. 2). The weather is clear and sunny, with a breeze strong enough to fill the sails of the three boats on the lake. Two scholars, one clearly seated at his desk, can be seen inside their houses, but in the mid ground, shaded by an open pavilion, two gentlemen are taking advantage of the good weather to have a picnic.

The painting is constructed of opposing diagonals, the strongest established in the lower left corner by a group of four overlapping boulders moving upward to the right. Their momentum is continued by a zigzagging bridge and is echoed by rocks at the base of the tree above. Trees in full leaf and houses occupy the central part of the foreground passage but at the top the theme of rocks, or, as in this painting, mountains, overlapping and building upward to the right, is reasserted. This strong rightward diagonal is checked by two mountain clusters in the background, which develop in a series of overlapping shapes upward to the left. In this painting, as in the previous work, color and repeated brush strokes create a decorative effect.

4 The Landscape, An Elder Brother
Okada Beisanjin (1744–1820).
Hanging scroll, ink and light colors on paper, 50 x 20¾
Inscription: The landscape is like an elder brother,
            Beisanjin, the artist.
Seals: Square intaglio ''Takoku.''
       Square intaglio ''Shizen.''
       Unidentified intaglio thread-character seal.
Published: Young, Martie W. *Asian Art: A Collector's
           Selection.* Ithaca, N.Y., 1973. Pl. 4.
Private Collection.

Okada Beisanjin's origins are somewhat obscure. The earliest mention of him in contemporary sources states that he was an orphan who, because of his knowledge of Confucianism, attracted the attention of a man by the name of Asaka Kiheiji and that the latter took they boy into his home and set him to work in the rice fields. Later Beisanjin went to Osaka, where he was hired by Lord Tōdō of Ise, first as a rice warehouse guard, a position which carried the samurai's privileges of sword and surname, and later as his personal secretary. In the 1790s Beisanjin passed on his position with Lord Tōdō to his son Hankō and devoted himself to painting and poetry-writing, along with his friends among the Osaka literati.

Beisanjin was a self-taught artist, who took much of his influence from the *Mustard Seed Garden Manual of Painting* and from the Chinese literati-style paintings he was able to study in Japan. The art name he chose for himself, *Beisanjin* or ''Rice Mountain Man,'' reveals not only his background but also his great admiration for the Chinese literati artists Mi Fu and his son Mi Yu-jen, whose family name is written with the same character.

Beisanjin was primarily a landscape painter although human figures do appear in his work. The motifs and subject matter of his landscapes were fairly constant throughout most of his painting career while his brushwork methods exhibited the most change. However, in the last five years of his life, Beisanjin began to work in a humorous style that parodied orthodox literati subjects in small-scale, colorful, single-motif paintings.

The Landscape, An Elder Brother, an undated work, was probably executed in the first decade of the nineteenth century. Its emphasis upon the human figures in the landscape, the rounded shapes of its rock masses, its forceful use of brushwork to achieve form and texture, and its free use of color identify this work with those Beisanjin did in his sixties. In the painting the eye is led upward and into depth by a series of motifs, beginning with the lush trees near the two scholars in the lower right. Then the eye flows along the diagonal of the scholar's stick to the dark area of rocks and trees on the left and continues upward to the richly colored rock overhanging an open pavilion. The thrust of this rock initiates movement downward with the sharp drop of the cliff. The overlapping of rock masses and the repetition of the tree motif unify the fore, mid, and background areas of the painting. Referring to the close union of the scholarly hermits and the landscape, the inscription lends balance to the painting by giving weight to the upper right corner.

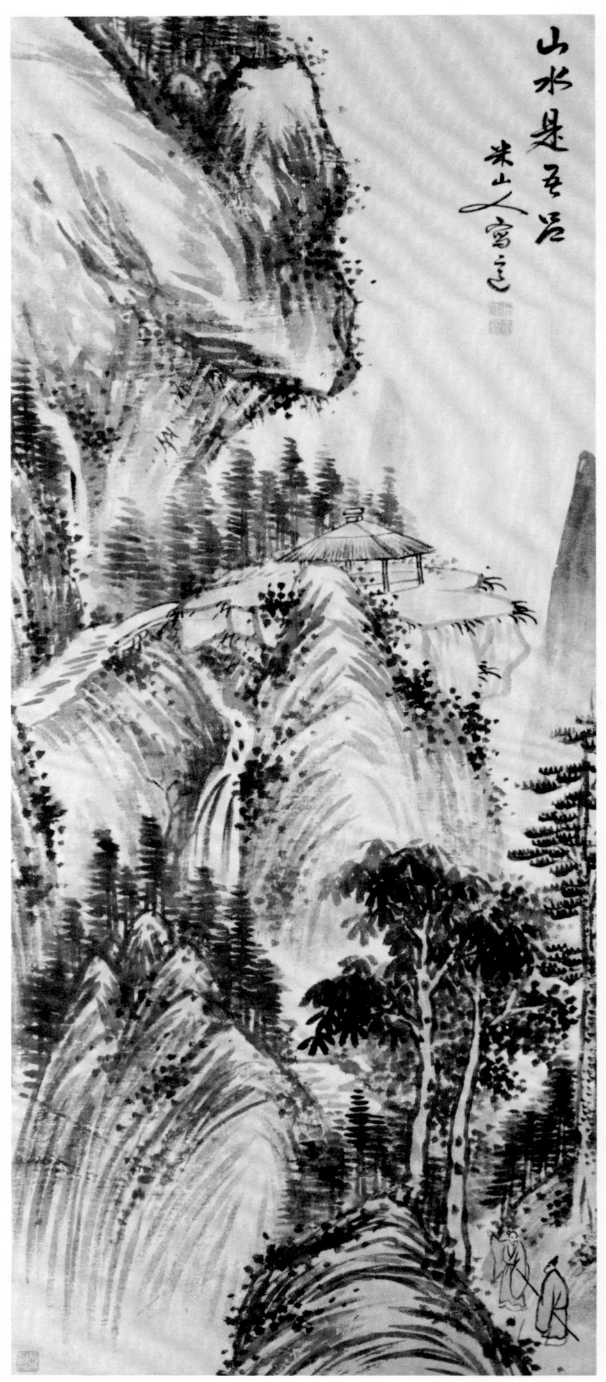

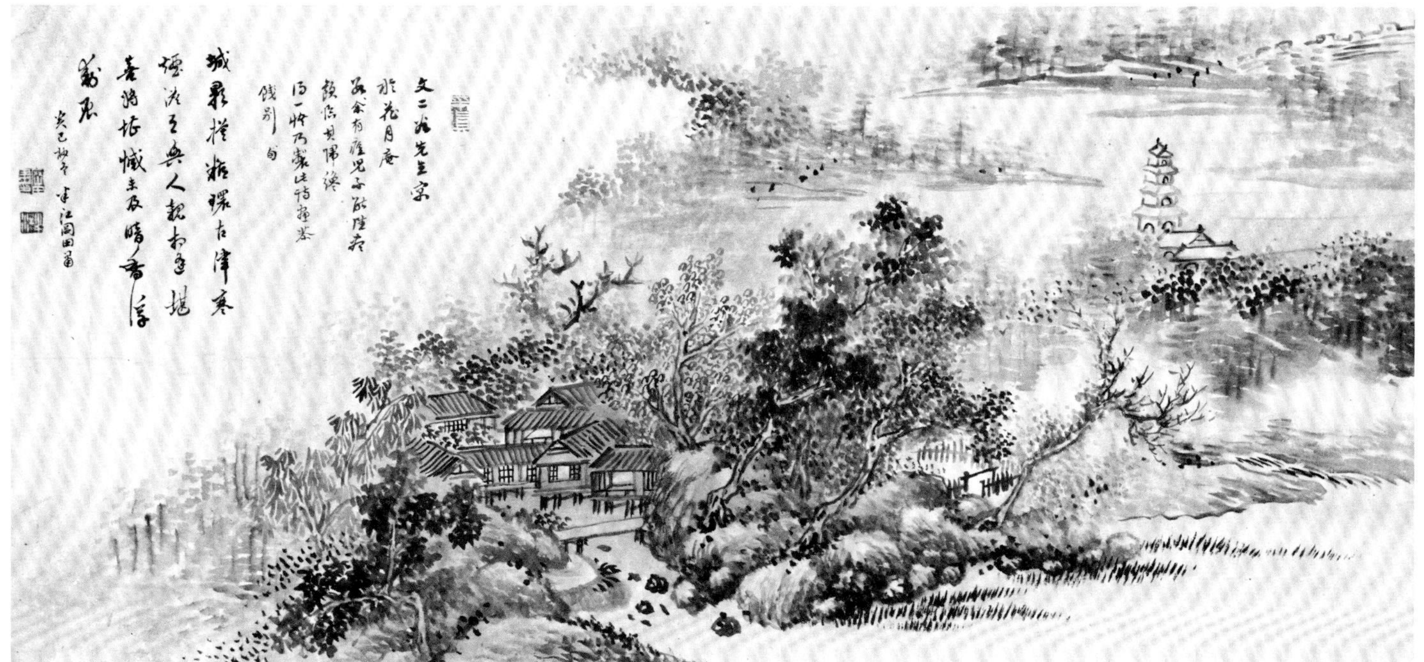

5   **The Farewell Gift,** 1833
Okada Hankō (1802–1846).
Hanging scroll, ink and light colors on paper, 11¾ x 31¾.
Inscription: The scholar Bun Nikoku had been living
    temporarily in the Kagetsu An (The
    Hermitage of the Flower Month)
    Because of my child who had been sick
    for a long time and would never get well, I
    could not see him until just before his return.
    I was able to visit him once and making this
    poem and painting I gave it to him as a
    farewell present.

    The blurred silhouette of the city is
    surrounded by an old harbor.
    The cold smoke and the pale sky participate
    in our intimacy.
    I am happy that we have met but soon I will
    be sad;
    Our visit will not last until the fragrance of
    plum blossoms wafts through the night.

Signature: Late winter of 1833, Hankō Okada.
Seals: Rectangular intaglio seal at the beginning of the
    inscription ''Saishin'' (True Appearance).
    Square intaglio ''Okada Shuku In.''
    Square intaglio ''Hankō.''

Collection: Mrs. Jackson Burke.

Okada Hankō, the son of Beisanjin, whose work is also represented in this exhibition, was a typical third generation Nanga artist. He began his study of painting with his father but later took his influence from the work of Yuan and Ming Dynasty literati, which was becoming known in Japan. His father disapproved of his painting, but Hankō nevertheless maintained his own direction, creating soft, atmospheric landscape paintings that depended primarily on the use of ink or colored washes to achieve their effect.

The painting *A Farewell Gift* is something of an exception in Hankō's oeuvre in that it is horizontal in format and emphasizes brush strokes rather than broad washes of ink. Furthermore, as the inscription suggests, it was created for a very specific occasion. The principal motif, a group of houses in a grove of trees, appears in the lower left of the painting, extending upward on a diagonal to the right. Pale orange is used to suggest the wood of the architecture and, at the same time, the warmth of human habitation, a theme that is repeated to the right in a tall pagodalike tower. The trees of the village are intertwined with mist, which like the group of houses, also extends upward to the right, to the very edge of the painting and to the motif of a city wall built along the ridge line of a range of low hills. The mood of the painting is positive—friends have gathered together to share their thoughts—but the grey mist encircling the village suggests the evanescent quality of the moment.

6 The First Visit to the Red Cliffs, 1826
Tanomura Chikuden (1777–1835).
Hanging scroll, ink on paper, 51½ x 14⅞.
Inscription: The prose-poem by the Chinese poet Su
            Tung-p'o entitled *The First Visit to the Red
            Cliffs* followed by Chikuden's own statement
            "Unable to stop musing about the past, I
            spread out a piece of paper and described
            my thoughts."
Signature: Chikuden Sei.
Seals: Rectangular relief seal preceding the inscription
            "Issho Senzan Sei."
            Oval relief seal following the signature "Chikuden."
            Square intaglio "Densha Ji" (A Country Child).
Private Collection.

Chikuden was born in Bungo, present-day Oita Prefecture, Kyushu, to a samurai family serving the Oka clan. Instead of following the traditional family occupation of physician, Chikuden became, by order of his clan, a Confucian scholar and teacher and eventually assumed the responsibility for the clan's school. A frequent, but unheeded, critic of clan feudal policies, he resigned his official position in 1813 at the age of thirty-seven, after his proposal for reforms to ameliorate conditions among the peasant class was rejected for the second time. Henceforth eschewing political matters, he turned to the literati style of life and engaged in such activities as painting and writing poetry. Prior to his resignation, Chikuden had studied painting with a local artist in Bungo and then with Tani Bunchō, whom he had met while on official clan business in the capital. In retirement Chikuden studied further with Okada Beisanjin, a member of the literati group in the Kyoto-Osaka area. However, Chikuden's style was influenced only slightly by his teachers. His most important source of ideas was the work of Ming and Ch'ing literati painters, which he had the opportunity to study in Japanese collections.

The First Visit to the Red Cliffs was painted in 1826 on the anniversary of and in an effort to recreate the image of the Chinese poet Su Tung-p'o's first excursion by boat to the Red Cliffs on the sixteenth day of the seventh lunar month. The choice of theme and its manner of execution reveal Chikuden's love of Chinese learning and his fondness for the refined sensibility so carefully cultivated by Chinese and Japanese who aspired to the literati life-style. The painting depicts the poet and a friend seated in a boat drinking wine and reciting poetry as they drift leisurely under the Red Cliff. It is night, and the light of the full moon that has risen above the hills suffuses the scene with a whiteness that merges water and sky. Chikuden maintains tight control of the composition by a careful balancing of vertical and horizontal elements. In the foreground the tall, narrow shape of the pine tree begins the vertical movement that culminates in the principal mass of the Red Cliff. Balancing the tree and cliff to the right, a massive rock formation, fills the left middle ground echoing the rounded forms of the Red Cliff. and in the background blurred, heavily-washed mountains check the

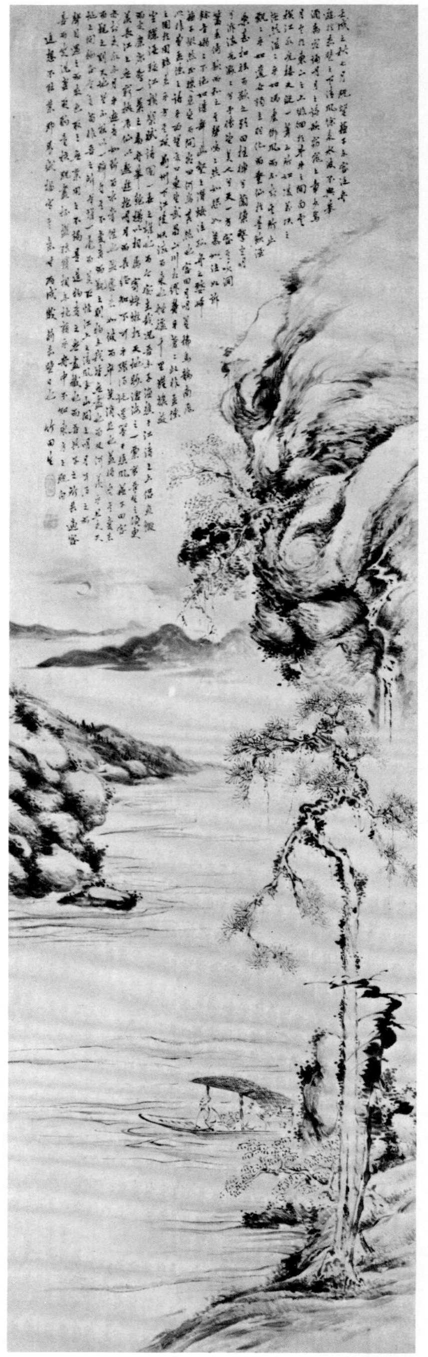

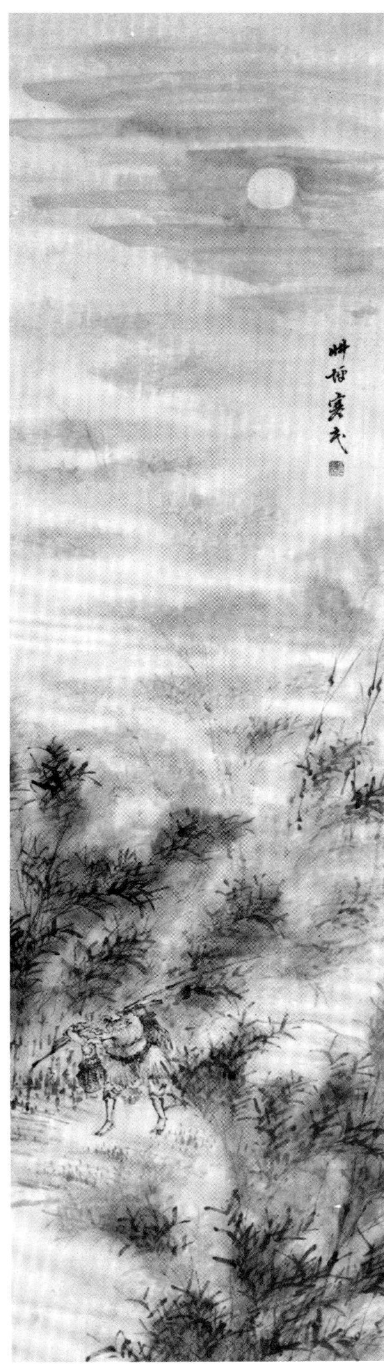

natural movement of the eye into depth. Chikuden's use of delicate brushwork and the gradual accumulation of soft strokes and fine, dry lines to build up images contribute to the success of *The First Visit to the Red Cliffs* by capturing the subtle poetry and emotion of the moment expressed in Su Tung-p'o's poem.

7   Fisherman Returning Home
Takahashi Sōhei (ca. 1802–1833).
Hanging scroll, ink and light colors on paper,
38⅛ x 10⅜.
Signature: Sōhei Kammin (Sōhei the Poor Man).
Seal: ''Tōi Rakushi'' (After This a Pleasurable Death).
Published: Young, Martie W. *Asian Art: A Collector's
       Selection*. Ithaca, N.Y., 1973. Pl. 11.
Private Collection.

Sōhei was born to a merchant family in Kitsuki, a small town in Bungo, present-day Oita Prefecture, Kyushu. The years of his birth and death are uncertain, but most art historians believe that these dates should be placed about 1802 and 1833. He was discovered at the age of nineteen by Chikuden when the latter visited Kitsuki and he quickly became Chikuden's best pupil. Chikuden thought so highly of Sōhei's talents that he was to comment some time later that Sōhei was more talented than his teacher. Sōhei frequently accompanied Chikuden on his trips to the Kyoto-Osaka area, where he met Chikuden's many friends and acquaintances among the literati. Shinozaki Shōchiku, a Confucian scholar in Osaka and one of Chikuden's closest friends, was so impressed by Sōhei that he arranged for him to marry his niece. Unfortunately Sōhei died before the wedding. Because of his premature death at the age of thirty-one or thirty-two, Sōhei never fully developed his own personal style. However, in his few paintings that remain, his talent as an artist is apparent.

In *Fisherman Returning Home* Sōhei has employed the soft wash style and the slightly humorous treatment of subject matter that Chikuden developed primarily for his album paintings, which are contained in such works as the *Porthole Vignettes* album of 1829. In Sōhei's painting an old fisherman walks along a moonlit path, his pole and creels balanced on one shoulder. Struck by the beauty of the evening, he stops for a moment to gaze up at the full moon. The utter simplicity of the scene and the humble status of the lone human figure give the painting a charming, ingenuous quality. In delineating the landscape the artist has used broad areas of wash, pale grey for the sky and darker grey for the forest beneath. To add definition to the trees, individual strokes of dark, wet ink have been applied over the wash. The fisherman, too, has been sketched in dark ink, but a pale flesh tone has been applied to his face, arms, and legs, and drier ink strokes have been used to suggest his scraggly beard and the straw skirt hanging from his waist. The contrast between the smallness of the man and the vastness of the mist-and moonlight-bathed scene around him conveys a sense of quietude and tranquility.

8   **Egrets and Lotus Blossoms**
Nakabayashi Chikutō (1776–1853).
Hanging scroll, ink on paper, 50⅞ x 16¾.
Signature: Chikutō.
Seals: Square intaglio ''Seishō no In.''
      Square relief ''Chikutō Sannin.''
Collection: David M. Okada.

Born in Nagoya Chikutō was the son of a doctor. Perhaps through his family's Chinese heritage, he became interested in painting and at the age of fifteen received the support of a wealthy businessman, Kamiya Ten'yū, who greatly facilitated his studies of the Chinese literati tradition. It was Ten'yū who introduced Chikutō to a slightly younger Nagoya painter, Yamamoto Baiitsu, with whom Chikutō maintained a life-long friendship. It is also said that Ten'yū gave both young men their art names, *Chikutō,* or ''Bamboo Grotto,'' and *Baiitsu,* ''Plum Leisure,'' taking as his inspiration two paintings in the temple of Daitoku-in—a bamboo painting by Li K'an and a painting of plum blossoms by Wang Yuan-chang. At the age of twenty Chikutō left Ten'yū's house to establish himself as an independent artist and seven years later, in 1803, he moved permanently to Kyoto.

    Chikutō is known today primarily as a landscapist, but like his friend Baiitsu he also occasionally turned his hand to paintings of birds and flowers, particularly water birds at the edge of a lotus pond. Within this format several approaches are possible: a realistic depiction in bright or subdued colors; an animated, monochromatic treatment; or an abstraction of forms through the use of contrasting brush strokes and various methods of applying ink. It is this last approach that Chikutō adopted in this work. At the center of the foreground area two water birds stand on thin, stilt-like legs. Light, rather dry brush strokes outline their feathers while the natural color of the silk has been left untouched to suggest the whiteness of their bodies. The lotus leaves around them have been painted with a brush unevenly dipped in pale, wet ink, the more heavily loaded part of the brush moving around the edge of each blossom so that when the ink dried, a thin, irregular outline would be formed. Finally, around the perimeter of the foreground passage and in the upper half of the painting, a lively rhythm of single ink strokes has been established, the sharply pointed fronds of reed grass below and the soft curves of willow leaves above.

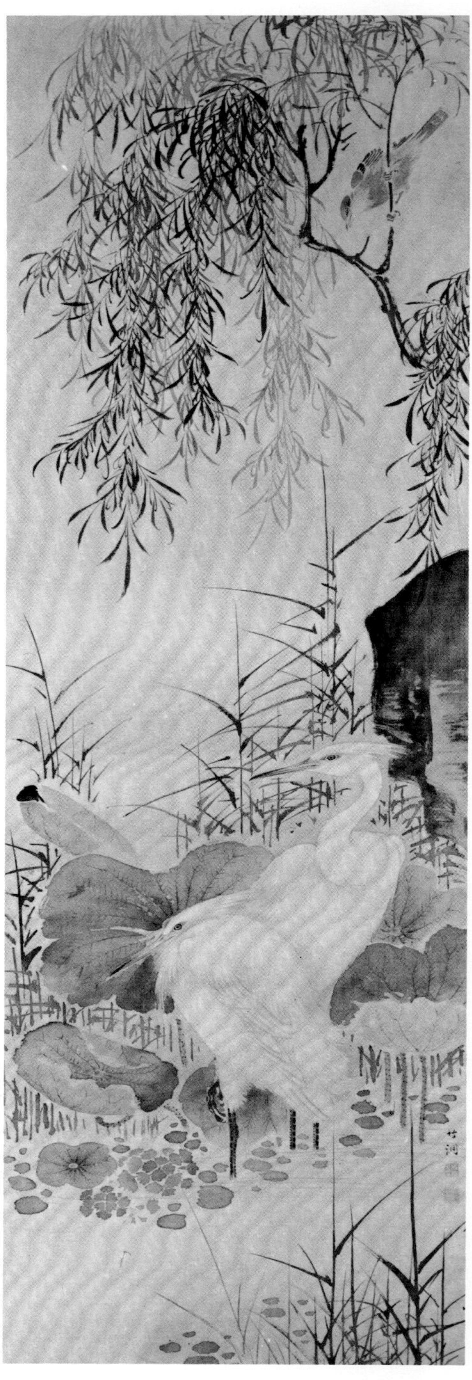

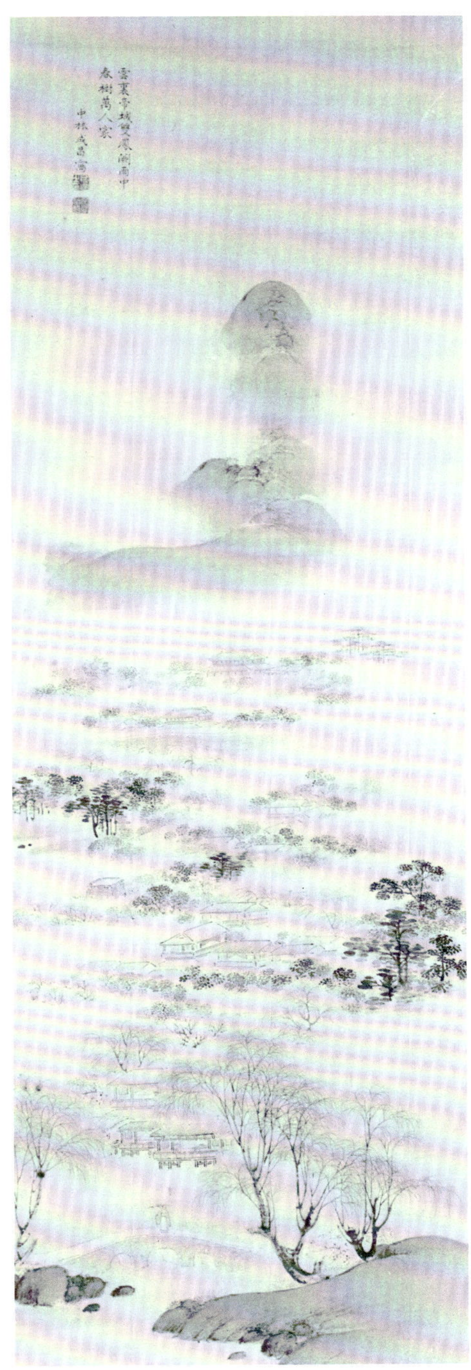

9   **Rain in Spring Trees**
Nakabayashi Chikutō (1776–1853).
Hanging scroll, ink and colors on silk, 36 x 12.
Inscription: Above the clouds a pair of majestic imperial palaces,
Amidst the rain, spring foliage and the houses of ten thousand people.
Nakabayashi Seishō.
Seals: Square intaglio ''Seishō no In.''
Square intaglio ''Ji Hakumei.''
Collection: New Orleans Museum of Art, Gift of Dr. and Mrs. Kurt Gitter.

Chikutō is known to have studied and copied many Chinese paintings, ranging from works in the style of the Sung painters Mi Fu and Mi Yu-jen to paintings by Ming and Ch'ing literati. At one time, it is said, his copies of the Chinese masters numbered 126 paintings. Precisely what the inspiration was for *Rain in Spring Trees* is not known, but several paintings in Western collections attest to the fact that in the late 1820s and early thirties—a period just following that in which the artist was known to have been actively involved in copying Chinese works—Chikutō began to experiment with broad, flat areas of colored washes distributed sparingly over the surface of his paintings. In the present painting color is used to emphasize the foreground shoreline and, to a lesser degree, the most distant mountains, thus creating a kind of color bracket around motifs depicted primarily in ink. Between these two areas of wash are clusters of delicately sketched houses, increasing in complexity of structure until above a masonry wall two multistoried palaces appear. The painting is a gentle but elegant evocation of spring created by the artist in middle age.

10   **Mountains and Valleys Deep and Far,** 1838

Nakabayashi Chikutō (1776–1853).
Hanging scroll, ink on silk, 36 x 12.
Inscription: Painted in Autumn, the ninth month, 1838,
        Higashiyama Sōdo, Nakabayashi Seishō.
Seals: Square intaglio "Seishō no In."
      Square intaglio "Ji Hakumen."
Collection: New Orleans Museum of Art, Gift of Dr. and
      Mrs. Kurt Gitter.

Although the title of this painting suggests a study of different types of perspective, the painting itself seems to deal with psychic rather than physical distance. In the foreground a scholar sits in a thatch-roofed pavilion gazing leftward, presumably at the lake over which his house projects. A grove of trees towers above the architecture, attracting the eye and encouraging it to move upward, while just above this grove a horizontal row of shorter, more distant trees arrests movement into space. It is as if the scholar's world is an enclosed one, even as his house is walled in, and he must cross psychic not physical distance to transcend his life's constraints.

Across a narrow body of water from the distant trees is another horizontal passage, beginning at the left with a bridge and ending at the right between the motifs of rocks and hills. The bridge is the slightly curved stone or masonry structure most frequently seen in Chinese paintings and may serve as the entry point into the scholar's fantasy world. Almost directly above the scholar's house appears an elaborate multistoried building adjoined by two corridors, which are supported on pilings above the water and which bow improbably around two groves of trees. Beyond, a delicate pagoda and the roofs of several other temple buildings can be seen. At the very top of the composition is a mass of dark, curving rock shapes, strangely undercut by mist. Though they are strong motifs that arrest the vertical thrust of trees and mountains, they are mysterious, insubstantial forms that complement the fantasy world spread out beneath them. The experience of viewing this painting is not so much that of movement into depth as psychic movement into the far mountains and valleys of China, the wellspring of the scholar's Confucian ideals.

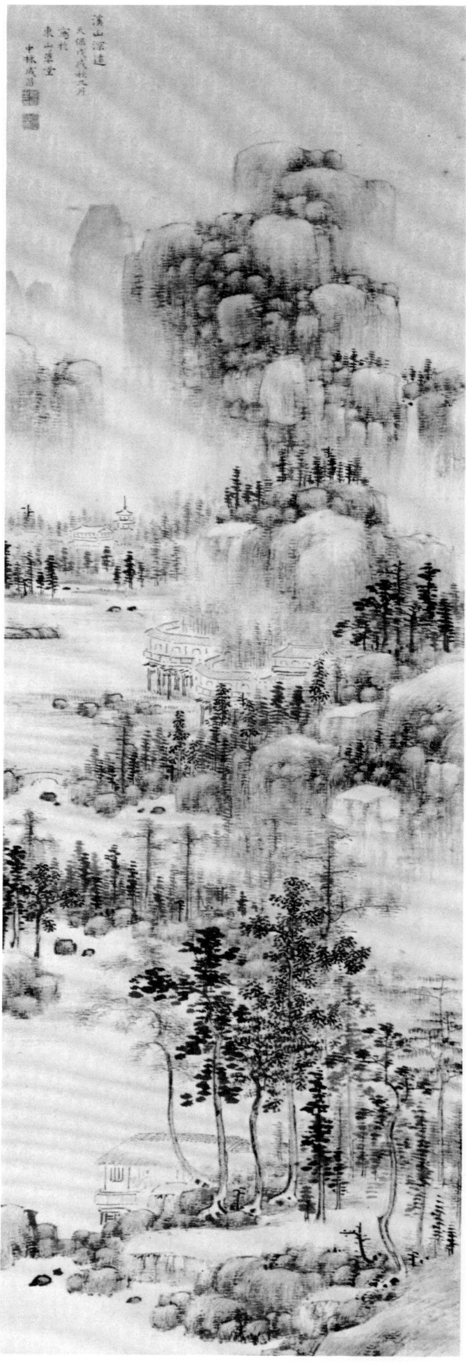

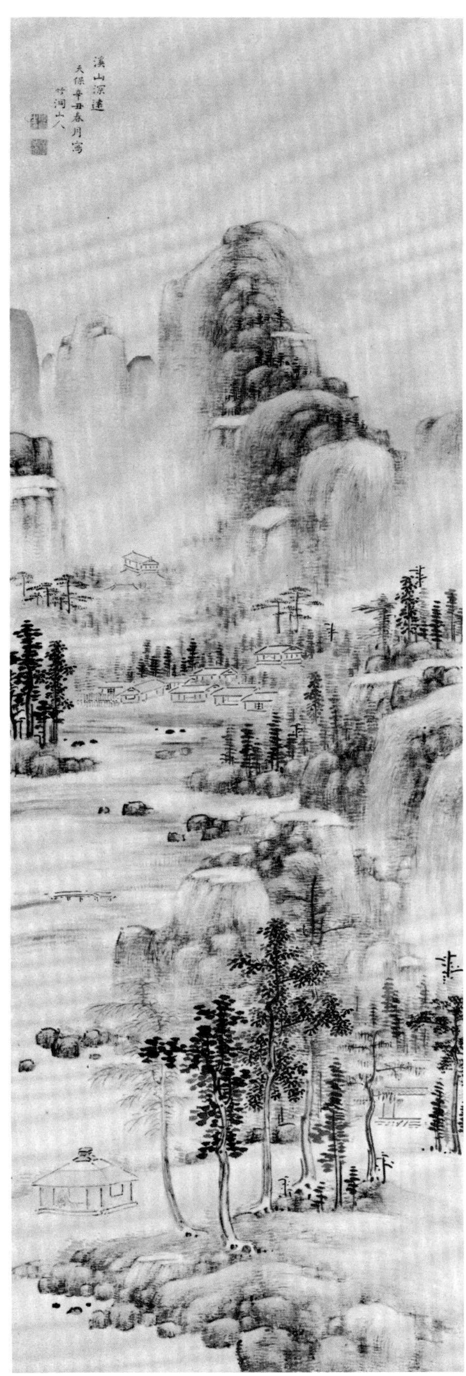

11   **Valleys and Mountains Deep and Far,** 1841
Nakabayashi Chikutō (1776–1853).
Hanging scroll, ink on silk, 51 x 16½.
Inscription: Valleys and mountains deep and far, painted
               in the Spring of 1841, Chikutō Sannin.
Seals: Square intaglio "Seishō no In."
          Square intaglio "Do Hakumei."
Collection: Yale University Art Gallery, Gift of Dr. and
               Mrs. Joseph Kurstin.

This painting, which has the same title as the previous work of 1838, is clearly a study of visual perspective. The elements of the composition are organized as a series of triangles projecting leftward from a solid base along the right edge of the painting. The first triangle, which begins in the lower right corner and projects all the way across the width of the painting, consists of an outcropping of rocks crowned by six tall trees and several smaller ones and a pavilion in which a scholar sits gazing out at the scene. The second triangle is comprised of a cluster of mountains capped with flat plateaulike surfaces and separated by smaller, rounded boulder forms that repeat the rock motif established in the foreground passage. The artist continues to build up his forms, beginning with pale washes which are occasionally coalesced into specific shapes by strong ink outlines, but more often this effect is achieved through the use of horizontal strokes in varying shades of ink. However, in the second triangular area the darkest ink tones are seldom used, giving the viewer a sense of the atmosphere blurring the more distant shapes. The third triangle is a negative rather than a positive form, increasing one's sense of penetration into depth. It is defined by passages of unpainted silk, by a stream of water between the shoreline and a group of dark, irregularly spaced boulders marking a diagonal (which is punctuated by a grove of trees painted in dark ink at the extreme left edge of the painting) and by a thin layer of mist appearing behind the trees and flowing upward to the right of the painting at the foot of the mountains. Enclosed within this triangle is a village of small, squat houses crisply defined with ink outlines. The clarity of this section, which uses a minimum of textural strokes, gives one the sense of a sudden glimpse through haze to an unclouded area. The background of the painting, the tall mountains, and a mist-encircled valley recapitulate the motifs stated in the lower part of the painting. Because of the relatively dark ink used to delineate these shapes, they seem to weigh upon the negative triangle, thereby checking the upward thrust of the composition. It is this area depicted in darker ink at the top of the painting—containing the clump of trees to the left and the grove of trees at the base—that creates a pattern of tones that unifies the many disparate elements of the long vertical painting.

12   View from the "Admirer of Mountains" Pavilion, 1844

Nakabayashi Chikutō (1776–1853).
Hanging scroll, ink on silk, 49¾ x 22½.
Inscription: Painted at Aisan Pavilion on Fugan in the
            Winter of 1844, Inshi Chūtan.
Seals: Square intaglio "Seishō no In."
       Square intaglio "Hakumei Ji."
Collection: Mrs. Jackson Burke.

In 1840, a year after the death of his wife, Chikutō gave his house to
his eldest son Chikkei and retired to a cottage in front of Shinnyodō
Temple, where he lived until his death thirteen years later. In spite
of the fact that this must have been a rather lonely period for him
since some of his closest friends among the literati had died—Rai
Sanyō in 1832, Chikuden in 1835—the last years of his life were
extremely productive and many of his finest and most challenging
paintings can be dated to this period.

View from the "Admirer of Mountains" Pavilion is a particularly difficult painting to grasp after the elegance of *Rain in Spring
Trees* or the spacial complexity of *Valleys and Mountains Deep and
Far* of 1841. The favorite Chikutō motifs are present: boulders,
round- and flat-topped mountains, clusters of trees, and the
ubiquitous scholar's pavilion. The familiar brush techniques may
also be found: washes over which dry outline strokes have been
applied and the horizontal "Mi-school" dots, which form a basic
element in Chikutō's repertoire. However, the motifs are concentrated in a single vertical just to the left of the median line of the
painting, and no attempt is made to suggest spacial recession.
Furthermore, the painting, being devoid of figures, lacks any obvi-
ous ideational content or human dimension. It is pure form and
texture, the work of an older artist with no one to please but himself.

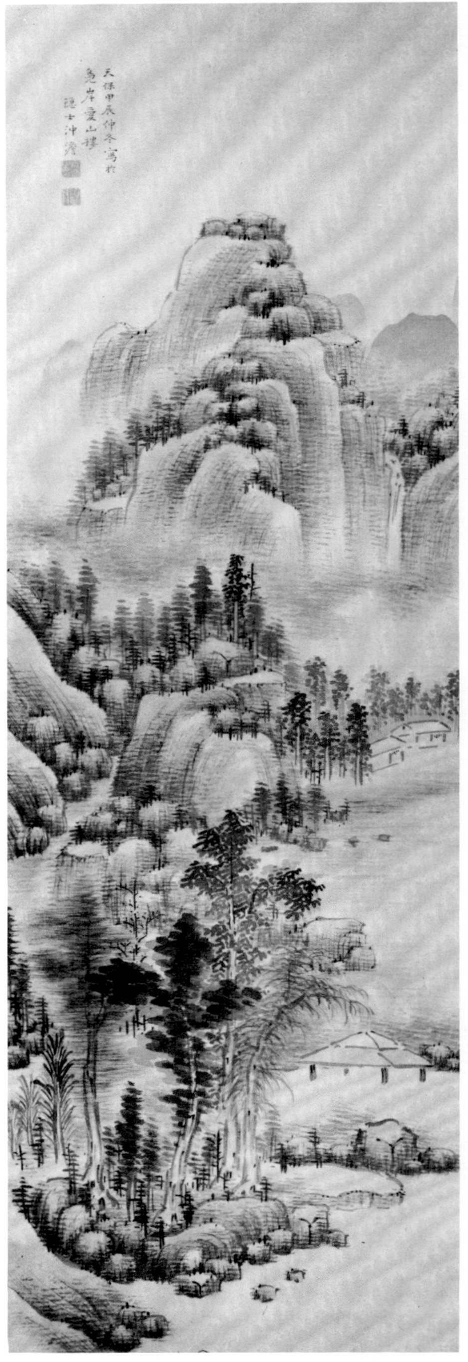

13 Heron and Lotus Flowers
Nakabayashi Chikutō (1776–1853).
Hanging scroll, ink on silk, 51½ x 16¾.
Signature: Chikutō Sannin.
Seals: Square intaglio "Seishō no In."
       Square relief "Chikutō Sannin."
Collection: Michael Fox and Robin Fox Cunningham.

In this painting of a heron wading through the shallow water at the edge of a lotus pond, Chikutō has created a work which has both the animation of a natural scene and the subtle contrast of brush strokes and ink tones that so delighted the sensibilities of the literati. The compositional framework on which the painting is constructed is a strong vertical made up of a cluster of elements—a single white heron; grey lotus leaves, one drooping into the water, others in various positions, their edges curving in space; and three lotus flowers, one a bud, another full blown, and a third whose petals have completely fallen. Establishing a rhythmic counterpoint to the central vertical are several types of plants—spikey reed grass and gracefully bent wild millet—curving to the left. However, the most dramatic motif moving against the central column of lotus plants is the heron itself, which strides agressively leftward, its sharp bill emphasizing the thrust of its movement. A final element, which softens the opposing forces of the composition and adds a further degree of animation to the scene, is the ink-dot technique used around the edges of the upper lotus leaves, conveying the impression of irregular, natural forms in motion.

Not Illustrated.

14   Egrets under Flowering Mallows, 1833
Yamamoto Baiitsu (1783–1856).
Hanging scroll, ink and colors on silk, 45¼ x 16⅛.
Inscription: Painted [at the time of the] Bon Festival,
             Summer 1833 at Ryūchi Shoya (probably the
             name of Baiitsu's studio), Baiitsu Yamamoto Ryō.
Seals: Square intaglio ''Yamamoto Ryō.''
       Rectangular intaglio ''Meikei.''
Published: Addiss, Stephen. *Zen and Nanga: Paintings
           by Japanese Monks and Scholars.*
           New Orleans, 1976. Pl. 63.
           Stern, Harold P. *Birds, Beasts, Blossoms and
           Bugs.* Los Angeles, 1976. Pl. 76.
Collection: Dr. and Mrs. Kurt Gitter.

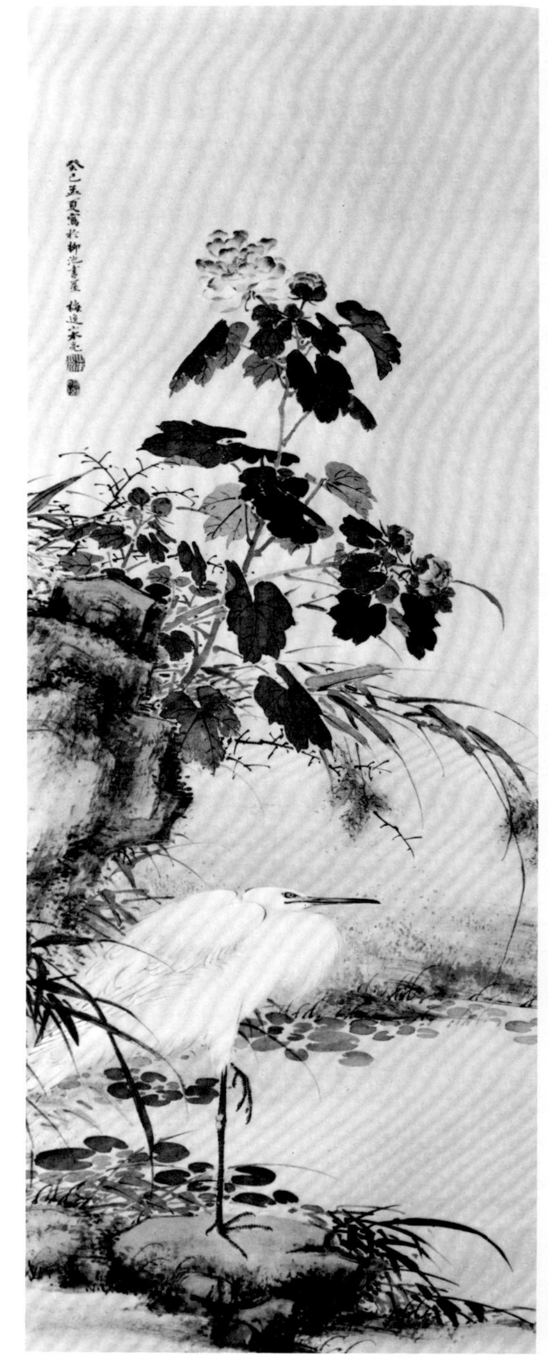

Baiitsu, an artist of extraordinary technical skill and versatility, is
considered one of the most accomplished of the third generation
Nanga artists. Born in Nagoya, he studied first with Yamada Kyūjō
(1747–1793), a practitioner of Nagasaki realism, and then with
Yamamoto Rantei, an artist of the Kanō school, and Chō Gesshō, a
minor Shijō school painter. At the age of eleven Baiitsu demonstrated his skill by decorating the *fusuma* or sliding screen panels of
a Buddhist temple. In his teens he met and became the protégé of
the wealthy businessman and collector of Chinese painting Kamiya
Ten'yū. While under Ten'yū's patronage, he formed a deep friendship with the young artist Nakabayashi Chikutō (1778–1853), and
together they studied the Yuan and Ming paintings in Ten'yū's
collection, as well as instructional texts such as the *Mustard Seed
Garden Manual of Painting.* In 1802 Ten'yū died, and soon after the
two friends left for Kyoto, where they joined the literati painting
group headed by Rai Sanyō. Baiitsu lived and worked steadily in
Kyoto for the next thirteen years. He then traveled to Edo but was
soon recalled to Kyoto, where he met and worked with Tani Bunchō on a new imperial reception room. Later he returned to Tokyo
with Bunchō, and together they formed the painting society called
''The Tower of Eight Hundred Perfections.''
    Baiitsu traveled extensively in the middle Honshu area and
gained more of a reputation for his decorative *kachō,* ''bird and
flower paintings,'' than for his quiet Nanga landscapes. His *kachō,*
produced in abundance, were delicately colored and superbly
executed in what was soon to be recognized as Baiitsu's own
inimitable style. Unfortunately, his contemporaries grew jealous of
his success and devised a scheme to humiliate him. It is said that a
certain geisha wore one of his paintings as an undergarment. Their
plan succeeded, and his reputation was tarnished. Two years before his death he returned to Nagoya, where he was subsequently
raised to membership in the samurai class by the daimyo of Owari.
    A man of extraordinary accomplishments, Baiitsu was a
master of the tea ceremony, a noted poet, and a skilled lutenist. His
extreme sensitivity, combined with exceptional talent, produced
an artist able to blend the soft, atmospheric qualities inherent in the
Nanga style with the harder, more sharply conceived linear quality
of the Kanō, Shijō, and Nagasaki schools.

This scroll, depicting an egret under flowering mallow plants, was painted by Baiitsu when he was fifty and is an example of his mature *kachō* style, which is strongly individualistic, yet soft and suggestive. The body of the egret is executed in spontaneous strokes with the feathers built up in a series of suggestive curves. Its legs and claws are sharply defined using a style similar to Chikutō's, a fact that suggests the possibility of a common influence.

Baiitsu possessed a remarkable sensitivity to nature. Using a wash method, he first painted in the leaf forms and before the ink had dried completely, he outlined them with a thin brush using various intensities of black. This method involves bleeding, which results in a gradation of tone and lends vibrancy to the leaves and plants. His eye for color juxtapositions was infallible as he blended delicate tones wet-on-wet in a technique known as *tarashikomi*. Finally, the pink of the flowering mallow adds strength and balance to the white of the egret's body, completing a highly decorative and satisfying composition.

15   **Landscapes of the Four Seasons,** 1848
Yamamoto Baiitsu (1783–1856).
Four hanging scrolls, ink on silk, 40½ x 19¾.
Published: Suzuki Susumu. "Yamamoto Baiitsu Hitsu
         Shiki Sansui Zu." *Kobijutsu,* no. 40 (March
         1973).
Collection: Mrs. Jackson Burke.

The style of the following four paintings owes more to Baiitsu's assimilation of his early training and his originality as a painter than to any single source of influence. The freedom of expression and freshness of creativity apparent in these landscapes represent a slightly different approach to what had become the traditional Nanga style.

Spring

Inscription: Early spring 1848, painted by Baiitsu Ryō.
Seal: Square intaglio "Yamamoto Ryō."

The gentle quality of spring is captured by Baiitsu's delicate brushwork. Tranquility pervades the painting—from the quiet, secluded pavilion under a gracefully bending willow to the group of houses across an expanse of quietly flowing water. In the middle ground the artist has introduced *haru gasumi,* "spring haze," as a means of diffusing light and blurring form. His use of overlapping motifs carries the eye up through the mist, and the almost vertical mountain range seems to float unsupported in the distance. The last fading rocky contour melts into the infinite distance, suggesting the limitless potential of the season of renewal. The bird's-eye perspective from which we view the scene creates a kind of spacial separation and the impression of an ideal world.

Summer

Inscription: Baiitsu Saku.
Seals: Square intaglio "Yamamoto Ryō."
        Round relief "Ryō."

If *Spring* is a gentle persuasion, *Summer* is a positive affirmation comprised of solid rock forms, some in shadow, some in bright sunlight. Baiitsu's technical ability, combined with a philosophical understanding of man and his role in nature, is especially apparent in this painting. The viewer is led into the composition by a diagonal formed by the convergence of water and land in the foreground, a frequent device in Baiitsu's landscape painting. On a small spit of land framed by a cascading waterfall, by deep cavernous rocks, and by lush greenery, two gentlemen-scholars are seated, a koto between them. One art historian has suggested that the men are listening to the waterfall after hearing the notes of the koto, but one might question this interpretation since it would be difficult, at best, to hear the delicate sounds of such an instrument so close to the roar of a waterfall. Baiitsu was sixty-five years old when he composed this painting, certainly not a dreamy, young innocent. He had seen his painting society dispersed and his reputation

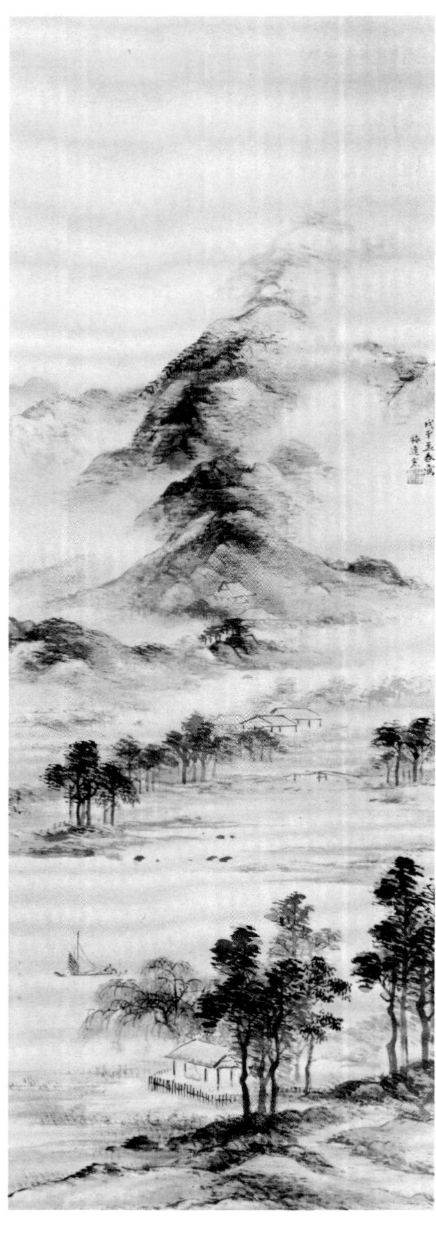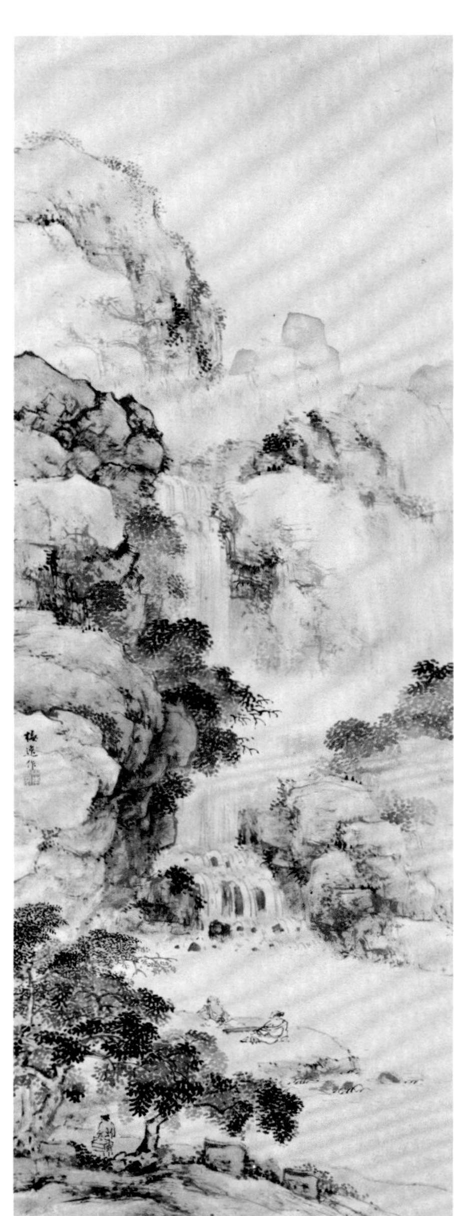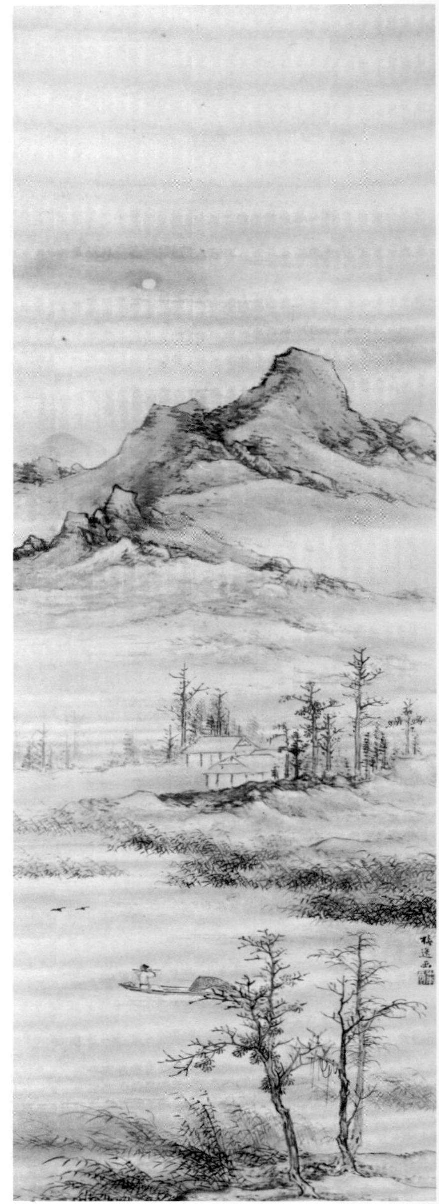

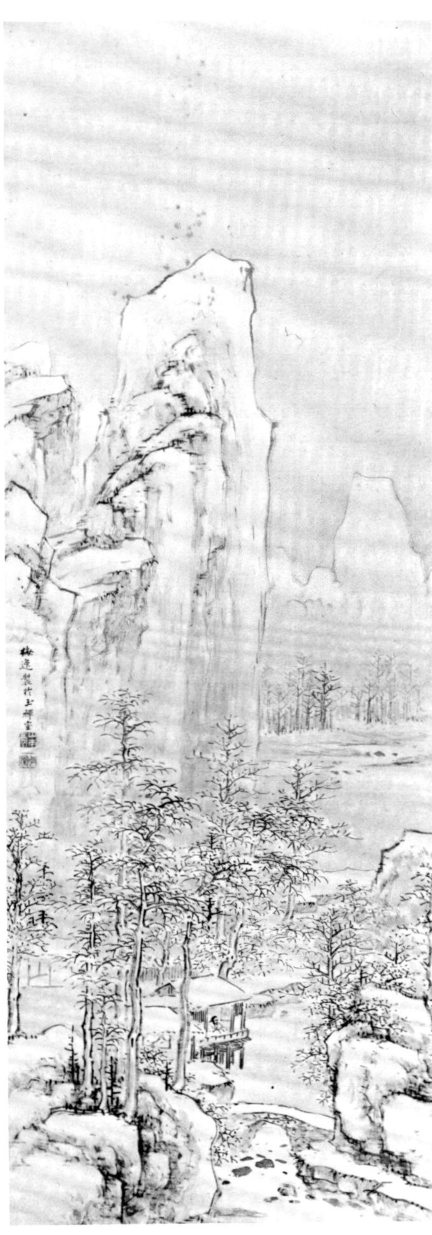

deliberately discredited. It is possible that he intended through the incongruity of this scene to give a satirical twist to his interpretation of the scholar's world.

Baiitsu's sensitivity to the potential of line is demonstrated by his masterly use of split and dry brush techniques. The soft, feathery lines, which give substance, as well as textural contrast, to his forms, are a basic element in his repertoire of brush strokes.

Autumn
Inscription: Baiitsu Ga.
Seal: Square intaglio ''Yamamoto Ryō.''

Leaving the lushness of *Summer* behind, *Autumn* is an embodiment of that season of change that brings to the fore man's own sense of isolation. The trees in the foreground have lost most of their leaves and tiny bamboos at the water's edge bend limply toward their roots. A figure playing the flute in a small boat is almost lost in the open expanse of water. Above, a harvest moon gleams distantly cool while birds fly south seeking a warmer climate. No mist nor overlapping hill shapes carries the viewer into uncertain distance as in *Spring*. Instead the upper half of the painting, comprised of moderately small, sharply defined, low mountains bare of trees or foliage, provides a passage of hard, uncompromising forms in contrast to the more lyrical quality of the lower half. This almost surrealistic barrenness represents a change in Baiitsu's style and first appeared in his work four years before the date of this painting.

Winter
Inscription: Baiitsu, executed at Gyokuzen (his studio in Kyoto).
Seals: Square intaglio ''Yamamoto Ryō.''
      Rectangular intaglio ''Meikei.''

Magnificent in its starkness, this painting is that rare instance of perfection in both its pictorial and atmospheric values. As in *Summer* the main figure, a scholar seated in purposeful contemplation of winter's silence, appears in the immediate foreground. The frozen lake beside his house is surrounded by stark rocks and leafless trees, which seem protective even in their frozen state.

The sharp vertical of the high-rising cliffs executed in strong positive strokes with a minimum of embellishments is further accentuated by the color of the background. The blue-black wash used to fill that distant area serves to outline and to contrast with the white of the unpainted, high rock formations, completing a picture of still, uncompromising cold.

16 Summer Mountains after Rain, 1854
Yamamoto Baiitsu (1783–1856).
Hanging scroll, ink and colors on silk, 59⅓ x 28¼.
Inscription: Painted in Winter 1854, a picture of summer
                 mountains following rain, Baiitsu Ryō.
Seals: Square intaglio ''Yamamoto Ryō.''
        Square relief ''Shinryō.''
Published: Addiss, Stephen. *Zen and Nanga: Paintings
             by Japanese Monks and Scholars.*
             New Orleans, 1976. Pl. 64.
Collection: Dr. and Mrs. Kurt Gitter.

Executed five years after the preceding set of four paintings, *Summer Mountains after Rain* utilizes a composition remarkably similar to that of *Spring.* The format is nearly identical, though a mirror image: the entry in the immediate foreground, the bridge in the mid ground, and the mountain range in the back.

In spite of the superficial similarity of these paintings, the composition of the later work seems to be creating a scene of overpowering, massive mountains carefully built up in a regular fashion, which eschews the easy grace and the brevity of stroke apparent in the earlier painting. *Summer Mountains after Rain,* executed in Nagoya, represents a distinct shift in style from Baiitsu's earlier work and may reflect the aging artist's increasing starkness of vision.

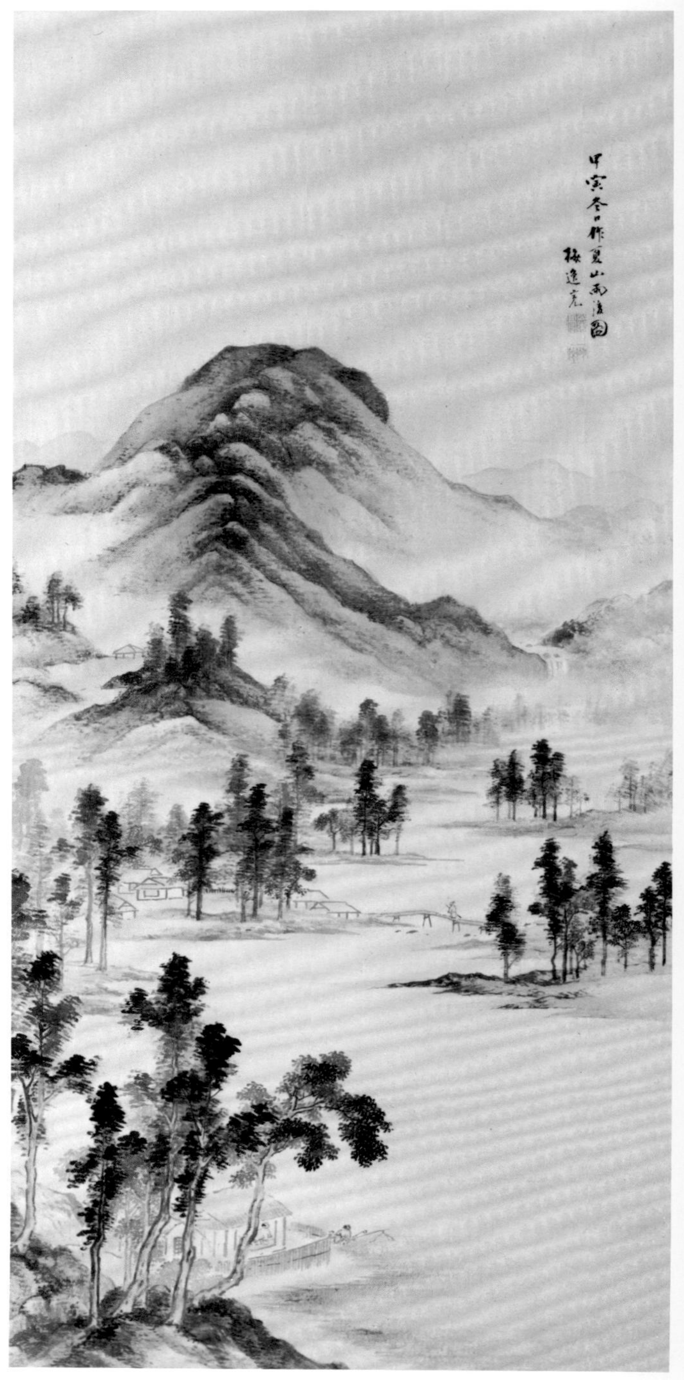

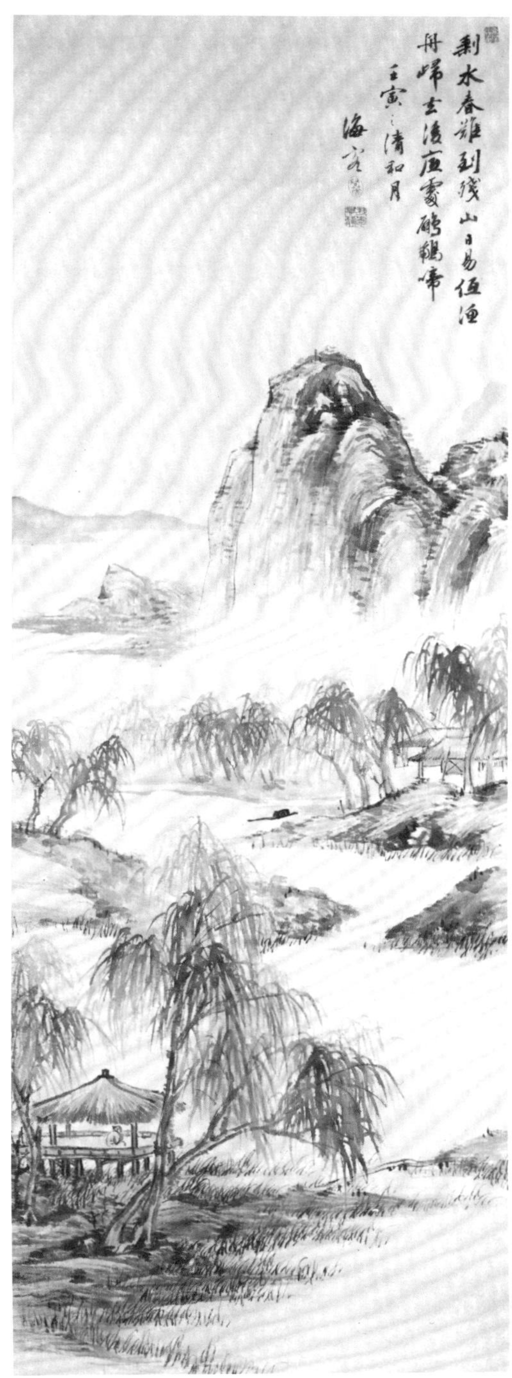

17 **Birds Crying at Dusk,** 1842
Nukina Kaioku (1778–1863).
Hanging scroll, ink on paper, 52¼ x 18⅜.
Inscription: Spring can hardly penetrate to this remote
backwater
The sun sinks down gently behind the
ancient mountains
After a fishing boat returns from afar
I hear the cries of a nightingale and a
shore bird
But where are they?
The second month, 1842, Kaikyaku.
Seals: Square intaglio seal preceding the inscription
"Kaioku Shiga" (Kaioku's poem-painting).
Oval relief seal following the signature "Kummo."
Square relief seal "Ga Ai Ki Sei."
Private Collection.

Nukina Kaioku was born to a retainer, an archery instructor on the Hachizuka fief, in Awa, modern-day Tokushima Prefecture on the island of Shikoku. Despite his parent's occupation, the martial arts were not Kaioku's forte, and at an early age he took up the study of Confucianism, painting, and calligraphy. At one point he traveled to Mt. Koya where he became interested in the calligraphic style of the Shingon patriarch Kūkai. Later he traveled to Nagasaki to study Chinese-style painting with the monk Hidaka Tetsuō. Returning to the Kansai area around 1828, Kaioku settled in Kyoto and opened a school to teach poetry and calligraphy. Although he produced a number of very accomplished paintings, which combine Chinese poems of his own composition with gentle evocative landscapes, Kaioku was best known in his own day for his Confucian scholarship and the excellence of his calligraphy.

In the painting *Birds Crying at Dusk,* executed when the artist was sixty-four, the principal motif is the figure of a scholar sitting in an open, thatch-roofed pavilion gazing at the water as dusk falls. His thoughts and perceptions of the world around him are conveyed to us by the poem inscribed at the top of the painting. Suddenly we realize that the scene in front of us, which at first seems grey and static, is actually rich in movement and sound—the sun sinking behind the ancient and weather-beaten mountain, the fishing boat plying its way through the water to its mooring, and the cries of birds in the shadowy marshes. Through the keen sensitivity of the scholar, we are able to experience much more than if we had looked at the scene unaided by his inscription.

The irregularity of the two willow trees to the left of the pavilion attracts our eye and constitutes a pivotal motif, which at once emphasizes the presence of the scholar and leads us further into space as we follow the contours of the willows and vertically projecting forms. In the mid ground two horizontal land masses, one capped by simple village houses, stabilizes the composition while the background, separated only by mist from the area in front, contains the ancient mountain mentioned in the poem and grey washes delineating other mountains in the far distance. The painting has an air of mystery about it. Throughout the grey ink tones suggest the early evening, a time when shapes loom large and colors and details visible in daylight disappear, a time when only the keenest of sensibilities can perceive the nuances of the surrounding environment.

18   Spring Thoughts While Watching a Fisherman, 1844
Nukina Kaioku (1778–1863).
Hanging scroll, ink and colors on paper, 53¼ x 27¼.
Inscription: Spring light suffused with green overflows
   the lake and shore,
   On the water a fisherman, on land a
   woodcutter
   and houses beyond the willow grove.
   Yesterday at Jo-yeh they gave me sake on
   credit;
   The skiff drifted back downstream on the
   reflection of a valley full of flowers.
   The second month, 1844, drawn at leisure,
   Kaikyaku.
Seals: Rectangular intaglio seal preceding the inscription
   "Kyōtō" (Capturing One's Fancy).
   Oval relief seal following the signature "Kummo."
Collection: Mrs. Jackson Burke.

In this poem-painting Kaioku has set down a group of visual images—willow trees, a river with a boat being poled through the water, and houses (both elaborate two-storied structures and simple village huts)—evoking a scene that, perhaps, he actually witnessed in the country outside Kyoto in the month of apricot blossoms, the second lunar month roughly equivalent to March in the Western calendric system. However, the scene is rather remote and impersonal. There is no scholar in the foreground acting as a surrogate for the viewer. Indeed, of the humans mentioned in the poem only the fisherman appears. However, although no woodcutter is visible in the painting, the words *fisherman* and *woodcutter* are frequently paired in Chinese poetry to connote a simple rural existence. With the introduction of the woodcutter image, Kaioku's thoughts leave the scene before him and move upstream to the wellspring of his intellectual interests, China. At Jo-yeh, a famous mountain in Chekiang Province, he is given a bottle of sake on credit. Does he mean that the wine of Chinese culture is something which the Japanese can only borrow, never truly own? The climax of the poem suggests its denouement. The poet envisions the Jo-yeh valley and its river turned to blossoms by the reflection of the flowers for which the valley is famous, all the while knowing that he is floating back downstream to the reality of spring in Japan.

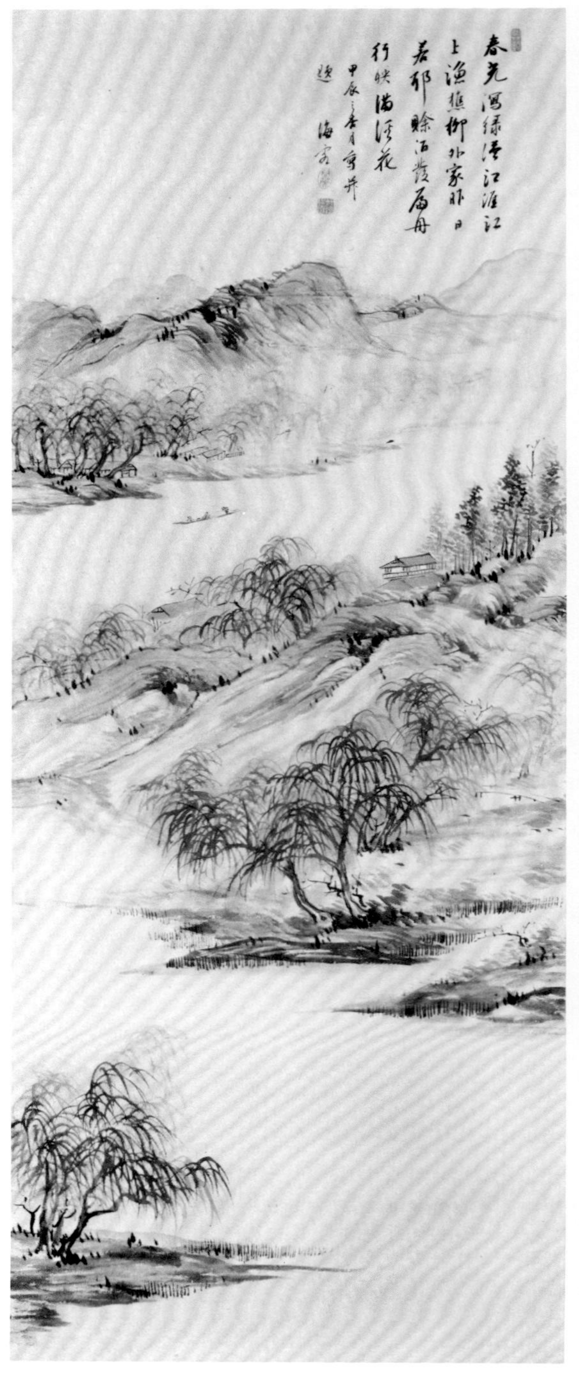

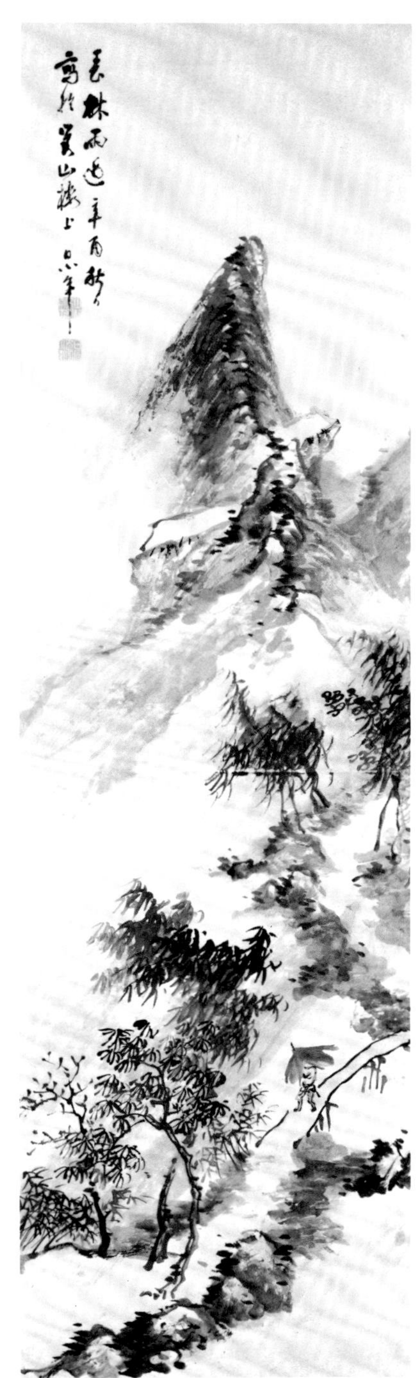

19   **Rainy Day in Autumn,** 1861
Hine Taizan (1813–1869).
Hanging scroll, ink on paper, 68 x 18¾.
Inscription: The forest rain has passed on an autumn
            day, 1861. Painted on top of Manzanrō
            (Taizan's studio). Hi Shōnen.
Seals: Square intaglio "Sansei Ji Taiko."
       Square intaglio "Nitchō jo Shōnen."
Private Collection.

Born in the village of Hine near Osaka, Taizan moved to Kyoto, probably in the late 1820s. Art historians disagree regarding Taizan's early artistic training, but all agree that he was associated in some way with Nukina Kaioku (1778–1863). He undoubtedly had access to Chinese paintings, though no one particular influence is evident in his work. Noted for his conceited and arrogant behavior even under normal conditions, when he was drunk he became obstreperous and frequently insisted that he had taught Kaioku, thirty-five years his senior, how to paint and that he had learned only calligraphy from his teacher. Another example of his egocentric nature is the fact that even when he was barely twenty he had the temerity to include his age along with his signature and the date of his painting in his inscriptions (according to Japanese custom, these acts were the height of arrogance and bad taste). Taizan's abrasive personality seems to have won him the disfavor of his colleagues in spite of their generally tolerant attitude toward eccentricity.

In this painting we see Taizan at his best in creating atmosphere and expressing force. Tonal relationships are built against the background of steep mountains and a winding path to create substance in the trees, figures, and mass formations. Using the traditional Nanga technique of overlapping forms, the artist draws the eye back into receding distance.

Sheets of rain, driven across the surface of the painting by unseen winds, form slashing diagonals of varying intensities. A small figure, bent forward and armed only with an umbrella, serves as a reminder of the insignificance of man against the uncompromising forces of nature. Perhaps in his own frustration Taizan saw himself as that small figure fighting against the almost overwhelming opposition of the world around him. His painting is a dramatic statement of opposing forces executed in controlled and masterful brushwork.

20 **White Sands, Green Bamboo,** 1862
Hine Taizan (1813–1869).
Hanging scroll, light colors on silk, 53 x 19¾.
Inscription: White sands, green bamboo, copied at the
              request of Shuntei Kentei at Manzanrō,
              1862. Hi Shōnen.
Seals: Square relief "Shōnen Shi."
       Square intaglio "Taizan Jin."
Collection: The Brooklyn Museum, Gift of Cr. Frederick
            Baekeland.

Taizan's inscription on this painting is more poetic than usual and
echoes the quality of dreaminess inherent in the work itself. The
traditional figure of a scholar resting under a shady tree makes the
rest of the painting appear to be a product of his reverie. The small
bridge over the wandering creek; a path; passing friends gathered
at the gate of a house, then continuing on through the trees: these
are the components of the scholar's quiet, uncomplicated world.
Suddenly the gently curving path changes in the middle ground
into a sharp zigzag pattern. This irregular shape disturbs for a
moment the tranquility of the scene, but above the sharply turning
path the soft mountain forms delineated in delicate color washes
restore the calm. Only the undefined, jutting rock mass on the right
side of the painting provides an uncomfortable terminus to the sky.
The occasional use of dry and split brush techniques gives definition to figures, trees, and other forms in the composition.

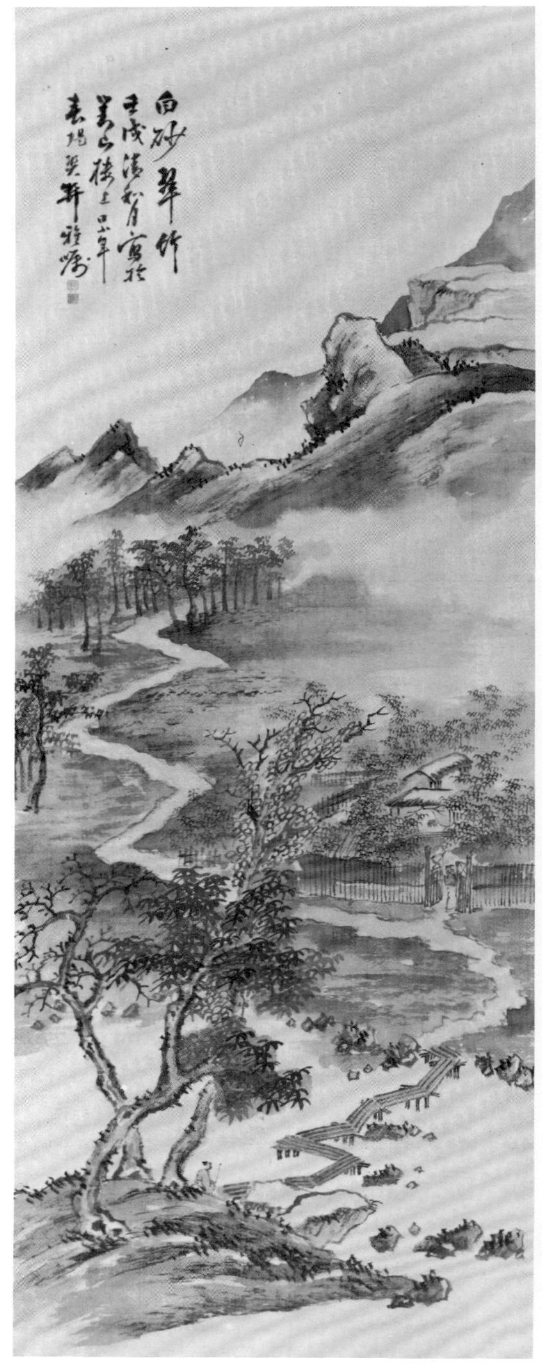